Aluminium Boatbuilding

SECOND EDITION

Ernest H Sims

ADLARD COLES NAUTICAL
London

CONTENTS

This edition published in 1993 by
Adlard Coles Nautical
an imprint of A & C Black (Publishers) Ltd
35 Bedford Row, London WC1R 4JH

Copyright © Ernest H Sims 1978, 1993
First edition published by
Nautical Publishing Company Ltd 1978
Second edition published by
Adlard Coles Nautical 1993

ISBN 0 7136 3691 2

A CIP catalogue record for this book is available
from the British Library.

Typeset in Century Schoolbook by August
Filmsetting, Haydock, St Helens.
Printed and bound in Great Britain by
Butler and Tanner Ltd, Frome and London.

PREFACE

This book is an updated version of my previous book *Boatbuilding in Aluminium Alloy*. Although much of the former edition remains relevant, welding machines and technology have now greatly improved. This makes it possible, once the machine settings have been accurately set, for a less skilled operator to obtain a reasonable quality weld, even though all important welds should, of course, still be entrusted to a coded welder. Anti-foulings have also changed, with TBT no longer being used.

A new chapter (Chapter 19) has been added on unit construction. This enables the smaller yard with limited space to build larger vessels, and helps the larger yard to employ more cost effectively more people at a time, thus reducing the time spent on assembly.

Finally, in order to broaden the base and make the book more complete, two new chapters, 20 and 21, have been added. Designing Structures in Aluminium Alloys is by Tony Marchant and Racing Powerboats is contributed by John Walker.

Tony Marchant has practised for over twenty years as a consultant in the marine industry, during which time he has been involved in the design of structures for many powercraft, fast ferries and sailing yachts. He is a recognised authority on lightweight structures for all types of marine vessels. He is a Director of the marine consultancy – Associated and Marine Technology.

John Walker worked with me as Team Manager for Enfield Racing. More recently he has been involved in building racing and fast power craft in GRP, FRP and aluminium with Cougar. He has charted powerboat racing as a competitor and journalist, currently for *Motorboats Monthly*, and is a director of the technical consultancy – Associated and Marine Technology.

Ernest H. Sims
1993

ACKNOWLEDGEMENTS

For the First Edition my thanks must go to the following:

To John Goulandris for providing me with the opportunity to experiment and to develop construction techniques which up to that time were totally unknown; to the members of the team at Enfield Marine Ltd who, by their ingenuity and perseverance, overcame some seemingly impossible problems – the fruits of some of which are recorded here.

To Tommy Sopwith who contributed a wealth of experience during his period as driver of the Enfield offshore race boats; his criticisms were always constructive and helpful.

To Don Shead and his team who provided most of the design knowhow; he was always ready with a sympathetic ear and a quick response to any construction problems.

To the British Aluminium Company technical department for reading the original manuscript, and making some valuable suggestions on corrosion.

My special thanks go to Jeffrey Please who provided many of the photographs; to my daughter Wendy who made such an excellent job of the typing, and to the following companies for providing information and illustrations:

Tucker Fasteners Ltd, Birmingham   International Paints Ltd
Insley Industrial Ltd, Bracknell   Alcan Ltd, Banbury

My thanks also to Erroll Bruce for his encouragement and patience. It took a lot of faith to publish a first off; I hope his faith was justified.

For the Second Edition my thanks go most sincerely to Kevin Leppard, a fully qualified practising welder, for bringing me up to date on the modern machines and welding techniques.

To the following for making available photographs of boats during the building process, as well as the finished product:

Eye Sea Library   Shead Design
Eye Sea Library/Cougar   FBM Marine Holdings Ltd
Eye Sea Library/Walker   SWATH Ocean International
Colin Taylor Productions   Souter Shipyard Ltd
Motor Boat & Yachting   Sims Aluminium Ltd

To the following for supplying photographs of the equipment used in production:
SAF Welding Products Ltd   International Paints Ltd
Gullco International Ltd   Eckold Ltd

INTRODUCTION

So much misconception and apparent mystery surrounds the construction, use and history of the marine applications of aluminium alloys, and so little advice or instruction exists, that this alone justifies adding yet another volume to the already bulging bookshelves of those whose livelihood depends upon satisfying the demands of the private and public sector for marine craft and ever-increasing marine applications.

There is little doubt that there is a significant use for aluminium alloys. The dilemma is: where, when, what and how. This book endeavours to answer some of the many questions still outstanding. It is not an exhaustive study, and it is presumed that the reader has a knowledge of boatbuilding. He or she may even be currently engaged professionally in supplying boats in the 1–40 m (3–131 ft) range, but is finding that certain customers' demands cannot be met by the use of existing practices. There are, unquestionably, types of craft and other applications where aluminium alloys will perform their function in a way that is superior to all other materials, just as wood, plastic and steel are in turn superior in their own specialist uses.

Because of the higher prices of the basic materials, an aluminium boat may initially cost more than a similar steel vessel. There are, however, savings to be made over a period of years that justify the increased cost and could even result in a net gain. It has been variously calculated that a weight saving of 35–45 per cent can be expected from the use of aluminium alloys as against steel for hulls, and 55–65 per cent for superstructures. The advantage gained by the weight saving can be capitalised by an increase in speed for the same engine hp or a reduction in engine hp for the same speed. Maintenance costs are considerably reduced; there is no oxide bleeding (ie rusting) when the paint film deteriorates or is damaged. An aluminium hull requires no painting other than for anti-fouling and for decorative reasons, and it will never be necessary to indulge in the time-consuming and plate-thickness-reducing task of rust chipping. If constructed of the proper alloys, an aluminium boat can be neglected to a far greater extent than those made of most other materials, provided that sacrificial anodes are maintained where dissimilar metals are in close association with the hull.

In the author's experience, it has been more beneficial to introduce those boatbuilders who use wood to the use of aluminium alloys than to use operators with an existing experience in steel fabrication:

- The boatbuilders using wood have a delicacy of touch that is not always in evidence in steel operators.
- Many of the tools of the boatbuilder using wood can also be used on aluminium, whereas few of the tools used for steel are suitable.

- Methods and techniques of shaping and forming aluminium differ fundamentally from those used with steel.
- Whereas with steel the effort is put into heating, hammering and forcing, with aluminium it is cold shrinking and stretching that provides better results. The material, being more ductile, responds to more gentle treatment.
- Larger bend radii are necessary for aluminium, and consequently different knives are used on bending machines.
- Welding machines and techniques for aluminium can be quite different from the normal welding for steel.

There are, of course, certain disadvantages in the use of aluminium alloys and these should not be overlooked, although the rate of imbalance is improving rapidly:

- There are still a great many more welding repair facilities for steel than for aluminium. However, on larger vessels, with adequate electricity-generating equipment, a small MIG or TIG set could be carried which would be sufficient for all but the major problems, or a shore electricity supply could be connected. A drill and a supply of rivets should be part of the boat's stores, which would enable at least temporary repairs to be effected (see Chapter 18 on repairs). A selection of various thicknesses of aluminium offcuts should be readily obtainable from the building yard, and it would be wise to have the building yard

FIG 1   *A 57 m (187 ft) motor yacht capable of 33 knots. The bow section is almost completed and is positioned ready for assembly to the midship sections. To date, this is probably the largest aluminium alloy motor yacht built in the UK* (Photo: Shead Design).

make up a repair kit consisting of all necessary items relevant to a repair of any kind.

- Aluminium has a fairly low melting point, about 593°C (1100°F). Consequently in high-risk areas, fire protection must be considered (see Chapter 16).
- There are certain items of marine chandlery that are not compatible with aluminium. This is rapidly being corrected as more and more fittings of a basic aluminium nature are becoming available; and, provided the proper precautions (as discussed in later chapters) are taken, even dissimilar metals can be used in proximity to one another without a disastrous effect.

Aluminium is a very clean material that does not involve dirty processes. It is comparatively lightweight, and therefore easily handled. Operators like working with the material, and the working processes of welding, cutting, drilling, shaping, forming etc are generally quicker than with steel – so production costs are lower. And although the cost of production equipment is higher, the effect of wear and tear is somewhat less. Saw blades are cheaper and last longer, and all cutting and drilling equipment maintains a sharper edge for a longer period of time. Cold shaping with the correct shrinking and stretching tools (see Chapter 3 on tools) is remarkably quick and effective, and storage of aluminium creates fewer problems than steel; there is less weight and less deterioration to consider.

When building in aluminium there are many thousands of sections for which extrusions dies are available. These include angles, channels, tees, zeds, 'I' beams, solid squares, flat bars, hollow rectangles, solid rounds, polygons, hollow hexagons, quarter rounds, beading, fillets, half round mouldings, step edges, corner mouldings, fluted strip and fluted angles, cover mouldings, water channels, drip mouldings, as well as a great variety of tube diameters and wall thicknesses. If a special extrusion is required, it is not expensive to have a die specially produced (depending on the quantity to be extruded).

A designer needs to prepare differently for the design of aluminium structures; design parameters and functions that have proved satisfactory in steel are not readily convertible into aluminium. The design criteria is different and should be recognised as such, just as the builder in turn must learn that aluminium is unique and that to obtain the maximum from it he must adjust to its own peculiarities and characteristics. The owner, too, has a part to play if he wishes to get maximum return from his investment. He must appreciate that aluminium dents and gouges more easily than steel, and must recognise the natural laws that exist in relation to the metal; these are all explained in this book.

1 ◆ Aluminium and its Alloys

The discovery of the element aluminium was made early in the nineteenth century. At first it was extremely difficult and costly to extract and isolating tiny particles of aluminium from the basic bauxite proved problematic. By the mid nineteenth century, though, the method of isolation changed. The new method used sodium instead of potassium, and enabled larger particles to be formed. Still later, this technique was improved upon when metallic aluminium was produced by dissolving alumina in a molten cryolite, obtaining about 22 per cent alumina; electric currents were then passed through the solution. As a result, the production costs fell dramatically.

The method of extraction widely used today is known as the Electrolytic Reduction Process. Fundamentally, this is brought about by the breaking down of alumina into aluminium and oxygen. Oxygen combining with carbon at the anode is released as carbon dioxide gas. As cryolite melts at around 980°C (1796°F) and the aluminium at around 640°C (1184°F), the process is continuous. It has been estimated that it requires about 20 000 kW hours of electricity to produce 1 ton (1.02 tonnes) of aluminium, and about 4 tons (4.08 tonnes) of bauxite to make 2 tons (2.04 tonnes) of alumina – with the whole process producing about 1 ton (1.02 tonnes) of metallic aluminium. During this process about 680 kg (1500 lb) of carbon electrodes are also consumed.

Thus it is clear that the production of aluminium is a highly complex and expensive operation. The most commercially pure aluminium has a very limited use: it is rather soft and weak, with a tensile strength of 4–6 tons per sq in. Its use is normally limited to spinning, and deep draws of a complex shape.

To produce a material that has the corrosion resistance of aluminium, but at the same time is commercially acceptable by having higher strength values, it is necessary to alloy various other metals with the aluminium – each introduced for a very specific purpose. This is called aluminium alloy.

There are many alloys of aluminium, and each is produced to fulfil a specific need for a specific industry. In this book, we will look only at those alloys that have a marine application.

Some of the metals used in varying proportions in the alloying process are: copper, magnesium, silicon, iron, manganese, zinc and chromium. Small percentages of these metals are used and vary according to the physical requirements of the finished product. For marine purposes, the greatest single element used is magnesium – comprising 4–5 per cent of the alloy. For most of the others it can vary between 0.1 per cent and 1.0 per cent. The remainder of the alloy is of course aluminium.

In general, there are two types of wrought alloy: non-heat-treatable and heat-treatable.

NON-HEAT-TREATABLE ALLOYS

The non-heat-treatable wrought alloys are indicated by the initial letter N. These alloys can be strengthened only by cold working and are softened by heating. The tempers or conditions in which they may be obtained range from soft or annealed temper to the fully work hardened condition. Temper is indicated by the following symbols:

O	Material in the annealed condition
M	Material in the 'as manufactured' conditions – eg as rolled, as extruded or drawn to size
H1, H2	Strain hardened material subjected to the application
H3, H4	of cold work after annealing or to a combination of
H5, H6	cold work and partial annealing in order to secure the
H7, H8	specified mechanical properties. The designations are in ascending order of tensile strength

It is normal to use the non-heat-treatable alloys in the O or M condition where much forming or welding is to be applied. As these alloys do not depend on heat treatment to achieve their mechanical properties, they can be reheated without any appreciable loss of strength. Also, they can be cold worked more efficiently than the heat-treatable alloys.

HEAT-TREATABLE ALLOYS

The heat-treatable wrought alloys are indicated by the initial letter H, and conditions are described by the following suffix symbols:

O M }	As for non-heat-treatable alloys
T	Material that has been solution treated and requires no precipation treatment
TD	Solution heat-treated, cold worked and naturally aged
TE	Cooled from an elevated temperature shaping process and then precipitation-treated
WP or TF	Solution heat-treated and precipitation-treated
TH	Solution heat-treated cold worked and then precipitation-treated
P	Material that has been precipitation-treated only

Thus a single heat-treatment alloy in its strongest condition is indicated by the suffix T, and a double-heat-treatment alloy by the suffix WP.

Heat treatment

There are three types of heat treatment that are commonly applied to aluminium alloys: annealing, solution treatment, and ageing treatment.

ANNEALING

A period of between $\frac{1}{2}$ hr and 4 hrs at temperatures between 350°C (662°F) and 380°C (716°F) is sufficient to soften aluminium alloys for cold working or to relieve internal stress. The longer times and higher temperatures are advisable for the medium- and high-strength alloys when maximum softness is required. The rate of cooling from the annealing temperature has a considerable influence on the final hardness. Cooling in still air is satisfactory for most purposes, but for the lowest possible hardness the material should be cooled in the furnace at a controlled rate of less than 20°C (68°F) per hour until the temperature is below 200°C (392°F).

SOLUTION TREATMENT

Solution treatment consists of heating for periods of between $\frac{1}{2}$ hr and 24 hrs at prescribed temperatures between 460°C (860°F) and 545°C (1013°F). The material is then quenched. The mechanical properties of most alloys are improved to varying degrees by solution treatment. The tensile strength and proof stress are considerably increased over the properties in the annealed condition, but the elongation is usually reduced. In comparison to the 'as wrought' condition, the improvement after solution treatment applies to all three properties. The temperature of the water of the quench has a considerable effect on the mechanical properties of the degree of internal stress. The cold water quench gives maximum mechanical properties, but the advantage is offset by the introduction of high internal stress. The boiling water quench leaves less residual strength and reduces the risk of distortion but the strength and hardness are lower.

AGEING TREATMENT

The improvement in strength following solution treatment can be further increased by ageing or precipitation. Some alloys begin to harden rapidly at room temperature immediately after quenching. Although the process slows down after a few hours, the maximum improvement in strength and hardness is approached after five days. For many alloys, ageing at room temperature does not produce the best properties and a treatment at temperatures between 120°C (248°F) and 215°C (419°F) is necessary.

The heat-treatable alloys, then, are the most difficult to form. But, almost because of that, they may be considered most suitable for longitudinals, stringers, etc, inasmuch as, because of their resistance to shaping, they may produce a fairer line, provided the shape is not complex or excessive. Even here, however, it is possible to provide local heat to aid severe forming. A good method is to use acetylene oxygen with a large, soft flame rather than the hard oxygen flame. Care must be taken not to concentrate the heat in one spot, but to spread it over a fairly large area. It is also possible that the strength properties would be affected.

The material considered by many authorities to be the most suitable for boat construction exterior use is, for plate, to British Standard Specification 1477 NP8 and, for extrusions, BS 1476 NE8. This is a magnesium alloy with the following characteristics:

Strength:	Medium (tensile about 18 tons per sq in)
Ductility:	High
Formability:	Very good
Corrosion resistance:	Excellent
Weldability:	Very good

For superstructures, a stronger sheet material could be used to advantage, such as BS 1470 NS6 H2 or H3, depending on the amount of forming. This has a higher proof stress, and would result in a stiffer panel in the thinner sheet gauges.

It should be, and often is, the responsibility of the designer to stipulate the type and grade of aluminium alloy to be used. Occasionally, though, the builder has to decide this, either because the designer has not specified it, or because the materials originally specified are not available and a substitute must be used. In these circumstances, the builder should have a good working knowledge of the characteristics of the various alloys and their conditions. The aluminium manufacturers are always very generous with their advice and literature, and you should take advantage of this.

Extruded panels

The recent introduction of extruded panels is finding more applications with the need for more lightweight structures. Time saving on welding can also be considerable. It consists essentially of a stringer, or web, being extruded integrally with the sheet or plate. This of course eliminates the need for securing the stringer to the sheet either by welding or riveting. Manufacturers are beginning to offer a wider variety of patterns, and some boatbuilders even have extrusions made from their own dies. Although light, the panels offer great strength, with economy on construction time. The inherent panel stiffness limits their use on curved surfaces, however. Their greatest value would be when used as decking and away from constant immersion in salt water. The panels are usually extruded in HE30 which only has a 'resistance to atmospheric attack' classified as good, as against the classification of 'excellent' of NE8.

For many years extrusions have been available for such areas as the gunwale, keel, chine and other specials, and there can be little doubt that the panels, with a little imagination, could prove immensely useful in many areas, including lightweight partitions, with many types of interior fillings; these are more fully explained in Chapter 20 (Designing structures in aluminium alloys).

2 ◆ DESIGN FOR CONSTRUCTION

This book does not attempt to cover the subject of design, which is discussed in various other publications. However, some naval architects unfamiliar with aluminium alloy construction will find it useful to have a knowledge of the practices used on the shop floor. Therefore an attempt has been made here to provide the designer with some background knowledge of how to exploit aluminium to its full potential, and at the same time to realise its limitations. (There is no point in the boatbuilder spending unnecessary hours trying to attain the impossible.)

To get the best results from using aluminium either in part or as a whole, the designer must be aware of its physical characteristics. In this way, he can design a structure for maximum efficiency. For all practical purposes, aluminium, like other metals, is of a homogeneous nature, and the physical characteristics of each different aluminium alloy are known and information is readily available from the manufacturer. It must be emphasised, though, that this applies in the 'as supplied' condition. In the non-heat-treatable alloys that are normally used for hull plates, heating has little effect upon these characteristics. But in the heat-treatable alloys, which to some extent gain their strength from a heat process, the characteristics can be affected adversely by the further application of heat.

The properties of aluminium compared with other materials are illustrated in Fig 2. These are general figures, though, and should only be used as such.

Because it is possible to design to precise safety factors and thereby produce a very light hull, it is all the more important that these safety factors are not eroded by action taken on the shop floor. This means that a degree of quality control should be specified by the designer, and that he should provide a large amount of detailed information to the shop floor. For this reason, and to familiarise himself with the problems met at operator level, the designer should spend, particularly in his formative years, as much time as possible on the shop floor. The process of 'coming up through the shop floor' has declined over recent years, to the detriment of the future designer. It is in the interests of everyone that, if a material is to be exploited to the full, the designer must be in a position to advise on shop floor problems (although he must not demand extreme or unnecessary standards).

Aluminium alloys have a high resistance to shock, provided that a notch or sharp change of section with its attendant stress concentration is avoided. This means that sharp radii, undercuts, abrupt change of section and other stress raisers should be avoided in highly stressed areas. It is probable that unsuspected stress concentrations and locked-up stresses are responsible for many failures, and material selection can do little to prevent such problems. Such stress concentrations cannot *always* be avoided, but designers should do their best to reduce their effects as far as is possible.

Material	Weight per cu. ft. (LB)	Coefficient of expansion $\times 10^{-6}/°F$	Modules of elasticity $\times 10^6$ lb/sq. inch	Approximate strength in tension tons/sq inch		Galvanic or chemical effect on unprotected aluminium
				Ultimate	Proof or yield	
Aluminium Alloy D54SM	165	13	10	17 (Min)	8 (Min)	None
Structural Steel (BS 15)	489	$6\frac{1}{2}$	29	28–33	16 (Min)	Mild
High Tensile Steel (BS 968)	489	$6\frac{1}{2}$	29	32–39	23 (Min)	Mild
Stainless Steel (18–8)	498	$9\frac{1}{2}$	29	35–45	14–17	None
Brsss (60–40) (BS 1949)	580	$10\frac{1}{2}$	15	20 (Min)	10 (Min)	Severe
Copper	556	$9\frac{1}{2}$	17	14–16	–	Severe
Phosphor Bronze (5% SN)	552	10	16	22–48	10–45	Severe
Aluminium Bronze (5% AL)	510	$9\frac{1}{2}$	17–19	25	–	Severe
K Monel (67 NI : CU)	554	8	26	31–62	11–58	Severe
Lead (Rolled)	710	16	$2\frac{1}{2}$	1	$\frac{1}{2}$	Mild
Zinc (Rolled)	445	22	6	10	2	Protective
Hardwoods	35–60	–	$1–3\frac{1}{2}$	2–15 (Comp)	–	Mild
Softwoods	25–35	–	1–2	2–7 (Comp)	–	Mild

FIG 2 *Comparative properties of materials.*

The prevention of fatigue is a matter of choosing the correct material and careful design. In fact, there is far greater scope for improvement in design than is generally appreciated.

Manufacturers of aluminium alloy provide figures for the mechanical properties of the various grades and tempers of their product, but it is important to define what these terms relate to. The tensile properties usually quoted are the tensile strength, the 0.1 per cent proof stress, and the percentage elongation. These terms are defined in BS 18:1962 as follows:

TENSILE STRENGTH
The tensile strength is the maximum load under the prescribed testing conditions divided by the original cross-sectional area of the gauge length of the test piece.

PROOF STRESS
Proof stress is the stress (load divided by the original area of the cross-section of a test piece) which is just sufficient to produce, under load, a non-proportional elongation equal to a specified percentage of the extensometer gauge length.

PERCENTAGE ELONGATION
The percentage elongation is given by $\dfrac{(Lu-Lo)\,100}{Lo}$

Where Lo = original gauge length
        Lu = distance between the original gauge marks obtained by measurement of the fractured test piece.

All designers will be familiar with the normal types of drawings that must be given to the shop floor in order for workers to do their jobs. However, there is

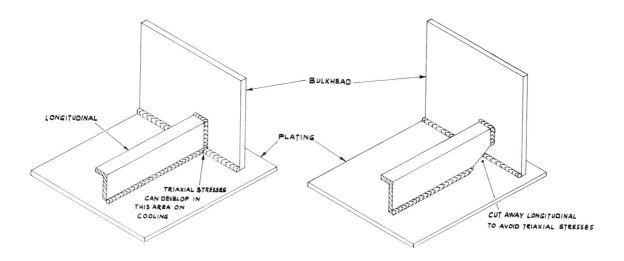

FIG 3 *Triaxial stresses in welding.*

one drawing that is sometimes overlooked, but is essential if the hull is to function at its maximum efficiency. This drawing is the shell expansion. It should indicate the precise location of all plate butts, giving dimensions from frames and bulkheads. These must not, of course, be located in areas of stress concentration. Stronger terminations should be shown where not continuous – ie when abutting a watertight or oiltight frame or bulkhead. Large-scale details should indicate where scallops are positioned to enable welding to be continuous and avoid triaxial stresses (see Fig 3). Waterways should be shown clearly. It is very difficult to cut waterways, ie scallops in longitudinal and transverse framing to allow bilge water to drain to a point leading to a strum box, after the plating has been positioned. The type of welding – whether it is continuous, staggered intermittent, chain intermittent, and the length of weld and gap – should be noted. Leg length and throat thickness of fillet welds and much other information should also be clearly laid out. It is unfair to complain of sub-standards when no standards have been given.

Welding symbols are fully covered in British Standards, and no doubt also in the Standards department of other countries, but unfortunately not all small yards are familiar with these expressions. This should be borne in mind when the general layout of drawings is being considered. The purpose of a drawing is to make a detail clear, not to confuse.

There are times when it will be advantageous to eliminate double curvature in hull plating. This can be achieved by using the multi-conic method of hull design. This will not eliminate any of the normal functions necessary in the production of a general hull design. Its only purpose is to modify slightly some of the sections so that a hull plate will simply wrap around the hull, because compound curvature has been eliminated. Not all designers favour this method, because it does somewhat inhibit choice of shape. The method is particularly useful for the design of moderately-sized chine boats. The various parts of the single sheet are laid out to bend suitably on cones of different ratios of height to diameter and, if properly laid out according to the principles of multi-conic projection, the edges of adjacent sheets will meet with a uniform welding gap. There are several methods by which the principle can be applied; the method described is not the most exact, but it is very simple. The reason why this simple method can be used on aluminium is that aluminium, at least in its thinner

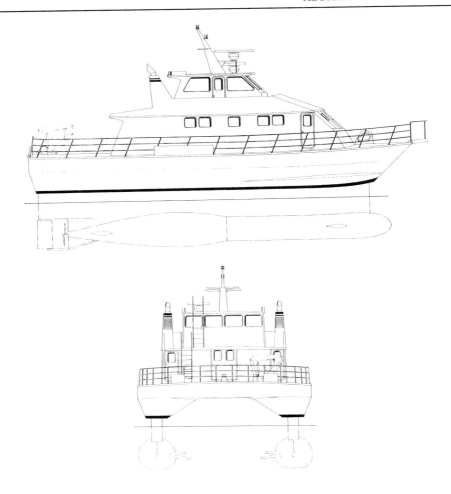

FIG 4 *Typical SWATH-type vessel. SWATH stands for Small Waterplane Area Twin Hull, which describes the essence of the hull form. The sea-keeping technique used in the SWATH places most of the buoyancy in pontoons well below the sea surface. Here the forces generated by ocean waves are small, having decreased exponentially with depth from the sea surface. At the surface, where wave forces are highest, the boat is kept as slender as possible.*

gauges, will naturally give a slight amount of double curvature. Plywood will normally give no degree of double curvature, and so a different method of projection must be adopted using a common apex for the cone with all generators emanating from it, or from a secondary apex situated on one of the original generators.

To use our simplified multi-conic projection, the designer prepares his lines in the normal way, by drawing the profile and plan views. We now draw in the radians. It is probably easier to start with the midship section, and the first bottom radian is drawn to the first or second station position forward of this (Fig 5). From the endings of the first radian, the chine, and keel to the chine, are divided into an equal number of parts, A to F and A' to F. These points are then connected with additional radians B–B', C–C', D–D', and E–E'. This equal spac-

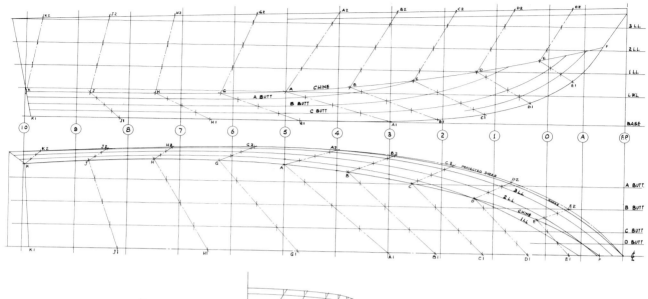

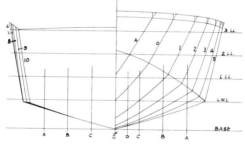

ing is for convenience only. From the profile these lines are projected to the plan below. Buttock lines are now drawn on the plan, and their intersections with the radians projected back to the profile. From these intersections the line of the buttocks may now be drawn. From the buttock heights in the profile, the shape of the bottom sections may be drawn in. (The aft body A to K is treated similarly.) To develop the topsides, the procedure is similar, but level lines are used instead of buttocks.

FIG 5 *Multi-conic projection.*

3 · Tools and their Application

Cutting

The cutting of aluminium is usually done either by shearing or sawing. For straight cuts on material up to about 6 mm ($\frac{1}{4}$ in) thick, standard power guillotines produced for cutting steel up to 3 mm ($\frac{1}{8}$ in) thick are suitable (see Fig 6).

Knife edges should be kept sharp, because blunt tools tend to burr the edges of a soft material such as aluminium. A clearance of one-tenth to one-eighth of the plate thickness is normal between top and bottom blade. Holding down pads on power guillotines designed for cutting steel should be exchanged for softer tops, usually made of plastic, as the harder type make indentations in the aluminium. This substitution can often be arranged with the supplier in the case of new machinery, and it is usually quite easy to fit the softer pads in second-hand equipment. The power guillotine should have a length of cut slightly longer than the normal length of plate to be used; this would vary from 1.8 m (6 ft) to 3.6 m (12 ft), but the average length of bed is a little over 2.4 m (8 ft) and the average length of sheet and plate is 2.4 m (8 ft).

Hand or foot guillotines are used for shorter lengths and thinner gauges, up to about 3 mm ($\frac{1}{8}$ in). Electric or air hand shears are very useful for sheets up to

FIG 6 *Power guillotine.*

about 2 mm (just under $\frac{1}{8}$ in), particularly for intricate shapes. Nibblers, both machine and hand held portable, are used on plate up to about 6 mm ($\frac{1}{4}$ in) thick.

Band saws (see Fig 7), preferably with a deep throat, are used extensively over a wide range of thicknesses. A narrow blade of about 1.25 cm ($\frac{1}{2}$ in) wide is used for cutting shapes, and a blade about 2.5 cm (1 in) wide for straight cuts. A skip tooth of about eight teeth per inch is satisfactory for average thicknesses of 3 mm ($\frac{1}{8}$ in) to 6 mm ($\frac{1}{4}$ in) – with slightly more TPI for thinner sheets and less TPI for thicker plates. Band saws should have a surface speed of 1524–609 m (5000–2000 ft) per minute, with the slower speeds used for the thicker plate.

FIG 7 *Band saw.*

If a variable speed saw is not available, the old-fashioned heavy framed type used for cutting wood is quite suitable. For cutting straight parallel lines in any thickness of plate, a circular saw with carbide tipped blades will provide an edge that requires no further preparation for welding. Lubrication of the cutting edge with paraffin-oil mixture, or soluble oils, will improve the cutting efficiency and increase the life of the blade. Where cutting has to be made in situ, or in the centre of plates, a portable jig saw is very useful; different blades are available for use on a variety of materials.

Routers can be used for cutting the most intricate shapes on any thickness of plate, and where it is necessary partially to reduce the thickness of a plate, a router is essential. Templates have to be made, and the setting up time is really only justified if a number of similar items are to be produced. For batch production, time saving can be very significant. A water-soluble lubricant should be sprayed on to the cutter to prevent tool pick-up and maintain the cutting edges.

Forming

Straight line bending of thin material up to about 18 gauge can be dealt with by the hand folder (see Fig 8); this is adequate for the task and easy to operate. For thicker materials without too long a bend, a hand operated flypress of suitable

FIG 8 Left: *Hand folder*.
FIG 9 Right: *Pressbrake*.

size (about No. 6) is used. All other bending requires a pressbrake (see Fig 9); this should have a bed of at least 2.4 m (8 ft) and be capable of about 80 tons (81.28 tonnes) pressure. When used by a competent and resourceful operator, a wide variety of shapes can be produced with a minimum of tooling. A multi-vee block, and about three segmented bending knives, with say radii of 3 mm ($\frac{1}{8}$ in), 6 mm ($\frac{1}{4}$ in) and 9 mm ($\frac{3}{8}$ in) would be adequate for most bending jobs.

FIG 10 *An aluminium alloy angle being formed into a ring on an Eckold Kraftformer KF460.*

Wrappers, ie lengths of thin aluminium bent around the knife edge, can be used for intermediate gauges. Choosing the correct knife for bending is dependent on the thickness of metal to be bent. Bend radii could vary from $\frac{1}{2}$ T to 3 T (T = sheet thickness). In practice, the material used in boat construction is fairly soft, usually O or M condition (see Chapter 1), so $1\frac{1}{2}$ T or 2 T is normal. A certain amount of 'spring back' is to be expected; the actual amount can only be found by experiment, so the punch or knife should have an included angle of about 86° where a 90° bend is required, to allow a slight overbend initially.

A very sophisticated tool for carrying out a variety of forming applications is the Eckold Kraftformer metal working machine (see Fig 10). Supplied in various sizes and operated mainly by a series of shrinking and/or stretching operations, the aluminium can be formed accurately to shape with a minimum of effort on the part of the operator. The largest machine has a deep throat that allows quite large panels to be worked. Two adjustable stops regulate the vertical movement of the pressure-adjusting ram and enable pre-selection of the most suitable working pressures to be made to close limits.

Tools are held in position by magnetic holders and are quickly changed simply by pulling one set out and pushing the next set in. A wide range of other tooling can be supplied for such operations as doming, flattening, shaping, planishing, bending, straightening, flanging, curving and beading.

Shaping

Cylindrical or conical shapes are produced on rolls, which are power or hand operated, depending on the diameter of shape and thickness of material. It is normal to use power rolls (see Fig 11) for anything above about 16 gauge, but if thicker materials are used on hand operated rolls it will probably result in distortion of the rolls.

There are normally three rolls arranged in pyramid fashion, with one fixed   FIG 11 *Power rolls.*

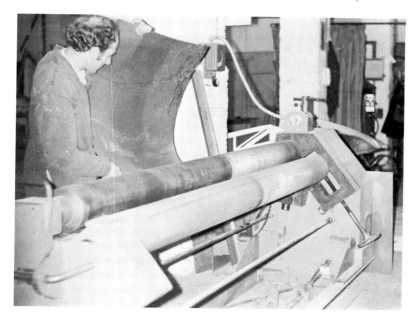

and the other two arranged variably, depending on the thickness of material and the required diameter of shape.

A hand operated type of 8.8 cm ($3\frac{1}{2}$ in) diameter × 1.8 m (6 ft) rolls and a 15 cm (6 in) diameter × 2.4 m (8 ft) rolls with 5 hp electric motor would be adequate for most boatyards. It is essential in all roll-forming that the surface of the rolls be kept in a clean, polished condition. When not in use, they should be kept lightly oiled and covered with protective paper. The oil and any debris should be removed before use. If pitting of the surface has occurred, protective paper should be used between the rolls and the workpiece.

Where double curvature is required in a plate, as in some skin panels, the planishing wheel is used (see Fig 12). The top wheel has a flat rim, and the lower one is shaped, depending on the curvature required. The workpiece is fed between the wheels to the area that requires shaping, then the lower wheel is raised so that the workpiece is under pressure and the workpiece is moved back

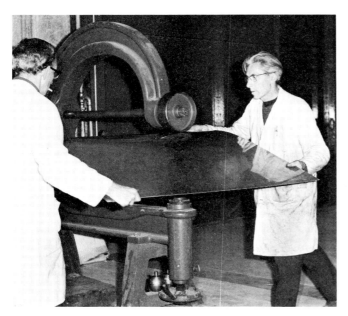

FIG 12 Left: *Planishing wheel.*

FIG 13 Right: *Shaping machine.*

and forth through this pressure area. This has the effect of thinning the metal locally and thickening it on the perimeter, which means that the centre of the panel has been stretched; the result of this is that the panel will have 'belly'. A degree of skill is required in this operation, but this comes with practice. It is much easier to put shape into a panel than to remove it, so a cautious approach is needed, with constant reference to the final shape – either the job itself or templates.

To shape extrusions or plate, a tool is needed with top and bottom jaws which grip the workpiece, and with movable sections in the jaws that can either press together laterally or press apart; these have the effect of shrinking or stretching the perimeter of the workpiece, which in turn produces an inside or outside curve. These machines are made in various sizes, depending on the gauge and size of extrusion to be treated. The smallest for use on up to about 1 mm ($\frac{1}{24}$ in) can be used in the fly press, and the largest can accommodate thicknesses of up to about 6 mm ($\frac{1}{4}$ in) (see Fig 13). The skills for operating these machines are

FIG 14 *A 11.4 m (33 ft) round bilge motor sailer. The judicious use of rollers and the Eckold shaping machine ensures a fair hull without any recourse to filling and fairing.*

quickly learned, and some complicated shapes can be produced within a very short time.

A certain amount of hand planishing or beating will inevitably be required. Wooden mallets, both pear shaped and round headed, have their particular uses, and are operated over a metal stake. This is sometimes referred to as raising. Mallets are usually made of box wood, but rawhide, leather, fibre, rubber and metal hammers are all useful. Tools and workpiece should always be kept clean and smooth as the soft metal is easily scratched. The grades of aluminium used in boatbuilding are usually of workhardening type, so the material should not be overworked. The number of blows should be kept to the minimum in order to avoid excessive hardening and cracking.

Aluminium generally is very ductile and, with the correct tooling, a little practice and gentle persuasion, it will easily respond to careful working.

Hand power tools

In a very small boatyard that employs less than six on the shop floor, the ordinary electric drills, etc commonly used for wood construction should prove adequate. When more than six are employed, a compressed air system that offers the use of pneumatic tools should be considered. Once installed, the savings are considerable and a large variety of tools can be served.

Where tools are to be used continuously, small electric motors fare badly, whereas air tools have very free moving parts and require far less maintenance. A compressor of adequate size must be installed, with power to spare for expansion. Particular care must be given to the layout of the installation, so that moisture, inevitably produced from the air during compression, is removed from the pipeline immediately before the air enters the tool, and at the same juncture oil should be introduced into the line. This is done by fitting filters and lubricators. This has the effect of reducing corrosion and automatically lubricating the moving parts.

Pneumatic drills of up to 6 mm ($\frac{1}{4}$ in) diameter capacity would normally have an operating speed of around 5000 rpm, thus greatly reducing the drilling time taken by electric drills.

Metal remover

Edge preparation for welding (see Chapter 4) sometimes makes it necessary to remove a portion of the inside faces of the butt joint (depending on the thickness of plate to be joined) to permit good penetration. For this purpose, use a carbide edge-cutter with guides either side, set on a mandrel which fits into a chuck or collet of a portable pneumatic tool, capable of about 25 000 rpm (see Fig 15). Where more than one pass is required in a welded joint, or when repairs are called for, it is necessary to chip back to sound metal. This can be done effectively and quickly by fitting the air tool with a vee-cutter that mills grooves in the weld metal (see Fig 16). Metal-removing burrs are also used in the same air tool; these have a variety of uses, and are available in many shapes (see Fig 17).

FIG 15 *Edge-cutter.*
FIG 16 *Vee-cutter.*
FIG 17 *Carbide burrs.*

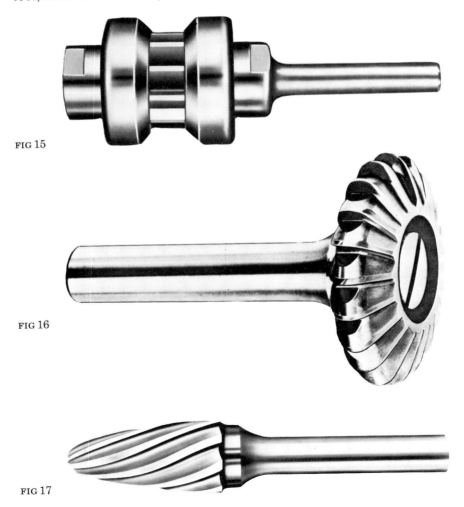

FIG 15

FIG 16

FIG 17

Rivet guns

Two general types of riveting tools are used. There is the reciprocating hammer type for use on solid rivets, where the rivet is entered from one side of the hole, a dolly is held under the head, and the tail is burred over with the vibrating punch. The other type is the 'pop' rivet gun, where the rivet is entered from the same side as the gun is operated, an extended mandrel in the rivet is gripped and pulled, and when the rivet is secured in place the mandrel breaks off. Both types of tool are air operated, and each type of rivet has a particular function (see Chapter 5).

Grinding

The standard type of carborundum wheel is not suitable for use with aluminium. Because of the softness of aluminium it quickly clogs the wheel and renders it useless. The most satisfactory results are obtained with the use of special discs spinning at between 12 000 and 15 000 rpm when fitted on to portable air tools. The discs are produced in various grades of grit, and are flexible (soft) types or rigid (hard). Great care must be taken, especially with the hard disc, not to dig the edges into the material; this causes ridges that are very hard to eliminate.

Grinding is normally used for metal removal on edges and excess welding. For strength reasons, butt joints on the skin should not be ground down flush, but a small weld bead should be left proud on the surface. The only exceptions would be where the owner demands otherwise for appearance's sake, or on the bottom of planing hulls where a smooth surface is essential to obtain planing speeds.

For finishing prior to painting, finishers or vibratory sanders are used. Some of these are fitted with water feeds so that sanding paper of the wet and dry type can be used, which increases the efficiency by reducing the tendency to clog.

4 ◆ WELDING

Only two methods of welding will be considered in this chapter: MIG (metal inert gas) and TIG (tungsten inert gas). Oxy-acetylene and metal-arc welding are not recommended for the magnesium alloys normally used in boat construction because of the poor joint efficiencies; this results in lower mechanical properties and corrosion problems. Only in very special circumstances should oxy-acetylene gas with a slightly carburising flame and flux be considered, and then only by an experienced operator who is fully aware of the dangers of not completely removing the excess flux after welding, which could result in serious corrosion problems.

There are two reasons why gas welding should be considered:

1 For butt welds in sheet that is going to be worked, ie wheeled or rolled. The resulting weld will be more malleable and will blend with a curve.
2 For urgent site repairs where the normal processes are not available.

Selecting the process

Whether you choose TIG or MIG for any particular type of joint or weld depends on many factors; the most important of these factors are the following ones.

PARENT METAL THICKNESS
This is described in more detail under the various process headings.

THE APPEARANCE
The appearance of the finished joint depends largely upon the quality of the pre-weld preparation and the welder's skill, but under equal conditions TIG is capable of producing a better-looking weld than MIG.

ECONOMY
Where large-scale production is called for, MIG is normally more economical than TIG. However, the amount of welding to be done will affect not only the selection of the actual process, but also whether you choose the manual or mechanised version of these processes.

DISTORTION
In general, MIG (because of its lower overall heat input), results in fewer distortion problems than TIG. The introduction of mechanised welding can also considerably lessen the problem.

The type of equipment will largely depend on the accessibility to the joint area. TIG equipment is less bulky, and the rate of deposition of filler wire is more easily controlled.

The TIG process

In the TIG process an AC or DC arc is struck between a non-consumable tungsten electrode and the workpiece, with the filler rod being fed independently. Fluxes are unnecessary as the arc itself cleans the electrode and weld pool, while re-oxidation is prevented by a shield of inert gas that envelops the area. Control by the welder of both heat input and the wire feed makes possible, in turn, a control of penetration; this is normally unobtainable with manual unbacked MIG welding. The TIG process is, therefore, normally favoured for un-backed butt joints that are only accessible from one side. Similarly, such precise manual control is an advantage where the weld path is complex. Welds to Class 1 standards and of the best appearance can easily be made with this process.

Manual TIG welding speeds vary from 12.7 cm (5 in) to 63.5 cm (25 in) per minute, and it is possible to combine the MIG and TIG processes to good effect. For instance, where a butt joint has to be welded, access is possible from one side only, and a backing bar cannot be fitted. A root pass could be laid down with TIG and subsequent passes, depending on thickness of parent metal, could be made with the MIG process.

TIG equipment

AC or DC units may be used. A composite unit that includes all the necessary auxiliaries is usually used for TIG welding of aluminium. However, a conventional AC transformer of suitable current capacity, and having a minimum open circuit voltage of 70 V, may be used if connected in series with a separate HF unit, a DC suppressor and a contactor as auxiliary equipment. An HF (high frequency) or surge injector unit is necessary for the arc to be struck between the electrode and workpiece without 'touching down'; this would contaminate the joint with tungsten and the electrode with aluminium. Should this happen, the tungsten-contaminated area must be chipped out and the electrode cleaned by grinding before welding can continue. A DC suppressor is necessary to give the required balanced current wave-form, which in turn will facilitate welding and improve weld quality.

The presence of a contactor in the electrical circuit is essential for safety reasons. Because aluminium welding uses higher open circuit voltages than steel, the supply must be disconnected immediately the arc is broken. The contactor does this automatically. While the above is true of older equipment, new TIG machines usually consist of a single piece of equipment that houses the AC – DC welding current supply and HF unit combined.

Torches for low-duty welding applications, up to about 100 A, are normally air-cooled, but water-cooling is necessary for high-duty cycles or greater currents.

TIG ELECTRODES

To minimise weld contamination, zirconiated tungsten electrodes are preferable to the thoriated type. Also, they have slightly higher current ratings and in general give rise to a more stable arc.

TIG FILLER RODS

TIG filler rod is supplied in straight lengths in various sizes. Rods must be of good quality and it is essential that they be cleaned before welding if they are supplied in the 'as drawn' condition when there is no subsequent cleaning by the manufacturer. This may be done with emery cloth. Colour coding on the tips indicate the filler alloy, and each manufacturer determines his own coding. Where the parent material is unknown, a cutting from the parent material may be used as filler rod.

GAS SHIELD

Argon gas of welding quality, having a minimum purity of 99.95 per cent, may be used for all aluminium welding, particularly for thin gauges.

Helium may also be used, and is especially useful for thick gauges where a faster arc travel speed can be attained. It also requires less edge preparation; thus the result is a higher-quality weld because of less porosity. Where a butt weld is made with passes on each side of the plate, the width of the overlap between the two weld passes is about three times greater for helium than argon. This allows a greater degree of latitude for misalignment between passes as a result of tracking errors. A mixture of argon and helium may also be used and where MIG argon/helium mixture is employed, wire sizes down to 0.8 mm can be used and provide a better weld. The preference of the operator, cost and availability all play a part in the choice of gas shield.

Fault finding of contaminated welds – TIG

The following items can be responsible for contaminated welds:
- Too much or not enough gas
- Incorrect torch angle
- Size of ceramic gas shield
- Too high a current
- Welding in draughty conditions
- Cleanliness of materials
- Using incorrect current (AC/DC)
- Wet or greasy plate
- Electrode too far out
- Arc length too long
- (AC only) welding without suppressor
- Incorrect filler wires

The MIG process

In the MIG process, an arc is struck between the workpiece and a continuously fed aluminium wire which acts as both the filler and the electrode. Fluxes are unnecessary. The arc itself cleans the electrode and weld pool while re-oxidation is prevented by a shield of inert gas, either argon or helium, which envelops the area. The filler wire feed is semi-automatic; wire is fed mechanically from the gun into the weld pool at a speed balancing the rate of burn-off, which in turn is determined by the current setting required for the weld. The arc is sufficiently self-adjusting for small movements of the torch, etc to be accommodated. A controlled arc system will be found to give additional control. Penetration cannot generally be controlled as closely as is possible in TIG welding so butt joints must be backed, or welded from both sides of the joint, except where pulsed arc is used. For manual welding, the spool of filler wire is mounted either separately on a wire feed unit ('ten pound' MIG) or on the torch itself ('one pound' MIG); the latter arrangement gives exceptional torch mobility and is especially useful for tacking. The small diameter of the wire (nominally 1.2 mm (just over $\frac{1}{20}$ in) or 1.6 mm (just over $\frac{1}{16}$ in)) makes possible a high current density, giving deep penetration, and welding speeds appreciably higher than those possible in TIG welding; consequently, with less total heat input, distortion is less likely. Manual welding speeds range from 33 cm (approx. 13 in) to 140 cm (approx. 55 in) per minute.

MIG welding is generally carried out with the torch held in the hand, and with the wire being fed automatically at a controlled speed; this means that distortion is reduced to a minimum. When a mechanised set-up is used, the arc length, rate of wire feed, and movement of torch are all controlled, the result of which is usually a far better weld – both mechanically and in appearance. The different MIG welding processes are identified by the manner of filler wire transfer.

SPRAY TRANSFER
Spray transfer is used for all positional welding on plate thicknesses from 1.5 mm ($\frac{1}{16}$ in) upwards. Expertise is needed on the part of the welder to control the weld pool from 'spilling over' on vertical or overhead runs.

PULSED TRANSFER
Pulsed transfer uses a combination of high and low current values. Basic machines change the value 50–100 times per second. More complex synergic-type machines alter the amperage and voltage setting to compensate for the welding technique, position and welder. The Kemppi PSS 5000 Synergic power source (Fig 19) is typical of this type of machine. The welder can change from MIG to TIG by selecting a switch on the panel. The current type DC + DC–AC is pre-selected for each welding method, so that when the MIG or TIG torch has been connected to the power source and the switch pressed, the required current type is automatically selected.

Synergy means you have control over arc adjustment. The wire feed rate governs the welding voltage in normal mode and the frequency in pulse mode. To sum up, the benefits are:

1 Simplicity of adjustment
2 Optimum settings
3 High reproducibility of welding parameters
4 Regularity of weld

Preparation for welding

Two conditions must exist before welding can begin. There must be a good set-up of the material to be welded, and the weld area must be clean.

All aluminium alloys of the type used in boat construction are covered with a hard tenacious oxide film. It is this natural covering that gives aluminium its corrosion resistance. If the film is removed by chemical or mechanical means, it starts to re-form almost immediately. While this oxide film is valuable in providing the corrosion resistance of aluminium, it does interfere with the welding process and must be removed before or during welding. The melting point of the oxide film is about 2020°C (3668°F). The melting point of pure aluminium is about 650°C (1202°F). Therefore, the temperature differential will allow the aluminium to melt before the oxide film. To some extent the oxide is removed by the arc during welding and the inert gas shield prevents its re-forming. A superior weld will result if the oxide film is broken up immediately before welding. This can be done quite simply by wire brushing the area, preferably with a stainless steel wire brush. An ordinary brush can be used, but this tends to contaminate the weld. The brushes should be kept clean and only used for this task; they should also be changed frequently.

Edge preparation

On butt joints of about 6 mm ($\frac{1}{4}$ in) thick plate and thicker, it is necessary to taper a portion of the inside faces of the joint to allow greater penetration. This is best achieved by using a carbide edge-cutter metal remover, as described in Chapter 3, or a planing machine, or even a dreadnought file, provided great care is taken to ensure a straight and even taper. Fig 18 indicates the general form necessary. Manufacturers of aluminium sheet and welding machines freely distribute to their customers excellent booklets covering the requirements for edge preparation for all types of joints. Experiments should be carried out using these tables and, where successful, they should be proceeded with. As experience is gained,

FIG 18 *Edge preparation.*

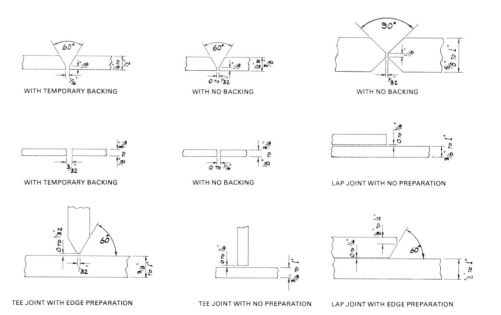

some welders may produce better results, with slight variations. This is only to be expected as no two welders weld in precisely the same way, and each develops his own technique.

Cleanliness

The need for cleanliness in the weld zone and surrounding area cannot be over-stressed. Any contaminates trapped in the weld pool will cause porosity, which will inevitably affect the mechanical properties of the weld. All dirt, moisture, grease etc should be removed with a degreasing agent. You need to choose one that will evaporate fairly quickly, such as white spirit or acetone. Cleaning swabs of a non-fluffy material should be changed frequently. Cleaning should be carried out immediately before welding. You need to ensure that your storage area is clean and dry; sheets should be stood on edge (preferably on wood battens), not too tightly packed, and there should be good ventilation.

Welding machines

There is a great variety of welding equipment available, manufactured in many different countries. Therefore you need to give very careful thought as to which piece of equipment you buy. Cost, although important, should not be your prime consideration. A piece of equipment that does not fully do the job you require is expensive at any price! Also, your future needs, as well as your present ones, should be considered. Some machines can perform a variety of tasks – dip, spray, and pulsed arc for instance – but it is still only *one* machine, and only one operator can use it at any one time. Obviously if that machine is out of commission for any reason, then all welding will cease. Thus it may be more important to have machines for each of the separate tasks.

A minimum requirement would be TIG, preferably with a water-cooled torch, for light gauge, tube, complex weld path, repairs, etc; a small MIG set, with air-cooled torch, up to about 200 A, for all light gauge work, positional welding, tacking etc; and a heavier MIG set with water-cooled torch capable of about 350 A that can be used for heavier wire and longer runs. When using water-cooled torches with water from a mains supply, a pressure-reducing valve should be incorporated – if not, after a very short time, leaking joints will be a constant source of annoyance. An alternative is to fit a self-contained circulating system incorporating a small lift pump and tank.

When deciding on your choice of manufacturer, consideration should be given to after-sales service and spares supply. Although TIG units are comparatively simple machines that seldom give trouble, MIG units are far more complex, and constant electrical maintenance is needed to ensure trouble-free operation and minimal down time. New MIG machines, though, require far less maintenance than some of the older ones.

Some welding plant manufacturers offer training facilities that are well worth attendance by new operators. It is no longer enough merely to stand alongside another operator to learn the craft. Most operators have some bad habits and these are easier to learn than to eradicate. There really is no substitute for practical instruction from a skilled demonstrator. Many manufacturers expend considerable effort developing new techniques, and so it is only sensible to take advantage of these offers.

FIG 19 *The Kemppi PSS 5000 AC/DC Multisystem machine, suitable for all types of welding: MIG and TIG.*

Fully automatic welding

There are many advantages to be gained from the mechanisation of the MIG process. These are: higher welding speeds, less distortion, and generally better welds as a result of controlled arc length and rate of travel. Pipe welding machines are used extensively where a high work through-put is required, but the capital cost would seldom be justified by the boatbuilder.

Plate welding machines for straight line butts can very quickly pay for themselves in time saved both in the initial welding, and by eliminating to a large extent the need for repairs to an inferior weld. There are two types of plate welding machine. The first is where the workpiece is brought to the machine, and the second is where the machine is taken to the workpiece. The former consists of a metal beam to which the plates are clamped, and an overhead carriage that carries the MIG torch. This type is normally restricted to a flat, straight weld path. The latter type can consist of vacuum track mounting system, whereby the track is secured to the hull by vacuum cups and the carriage carrying the welding gun is mounted on the track. The traction speed is variable, as is the wire feed (see Fig 20).

Multi-pass welds

More than one-pass welds may be necessary in plate of 6 mm ($\frac{1}{4}$ in) thick and over, particularly where manual as opposed to machine welding is employed. Before a weld is laid on top of another, it is necessary to remove the dross formed by the initial bead. This function is performed by backchipping with the pneumatic tool fitted with a vee-cutter, as mentioned in Chapter 2 (see Fig 16). It can be easily seen when sound metal is exposed. It is important to allow previous run to cool to approximately 120°C (248°F) before overpassing, and this can be accomplished by the appropriate use of heat crayons.

Plasma-arc

Plasma-arc welding and cutting is essentially an extension of the TIG process, using a mixture of argon and hydrogen gases. This welding process is claimed to improve the quality of the weld, with a greater tolerance of varying arc length, a greater degree of weld penetration, higher welding speeds, and reduced risk of electrode contamination. The rate of distortion is also reduced because of the narrow plasma arc, reducing the width of the heatspread to the workpiece.

Plasma cutting is a very efficient method of cutting most metals up to about 3.8 cm ($1\frac{1}{2}$ in) thick, including stainless steel. This results in a good clean edge that requires very little attention for a weld preparation finish. The cutting agent is a high-speed jet of gas, heated to temperatures up to 16 648°C (30 000°F) by an electric arc. Although the gas mixture will give a better-quality cut, compressed air is often used and will cut anything that conducts electricity up to 3.8 cm ($1\frac{1}{2}$ in) in thickness.

Run on–run off plates

These are extra pieces of parent metal tacked to the beginning and ending of the weld joint. They are particularly useful where no trimming allowance is possible. When starting a weld, a little time is taken to achieve full penetration, and at the termination a crater is formed. It is better that these deficiencies should occur on waste material, which is later removed.

Backing bars

Where a MIG butt weld is to be used and the back of the weld is accessible, it is usual to fit a backing bar. The value of this backing is that it prevents the force of the MIG arc from blowing through the joint. Where edge preparation is provided, and a small gap is made at the root of the joint, full penetration can be assured. A backing bar can take one of two forms, permanent or temporary. Permanent backers are strips similar to the parent metal, welded to the back of the joint. It is necessary to fuse the two edges of the joint to the backing strip, so a root opening greater than that used with a temporary backer should be allowed (see Fig 21).

Temporary backers (see Fig 22) are usually of steel or stainless steel and are grooved to allow an underbead of metal to protrude below the joint. This ensures full penetration. The groove may be quite shallow, between 0.75 mm ($\frac{1}{32}$ in) and 1.5 mm ($\frac{1}{16}$ in) deep, and wide enough not to restrict the edges of the bead. The shape of the groove is usually rounded, but it may sometimes be rectangular. The area of the joint must be firmly secured to the backing bar by clamping or bolting.

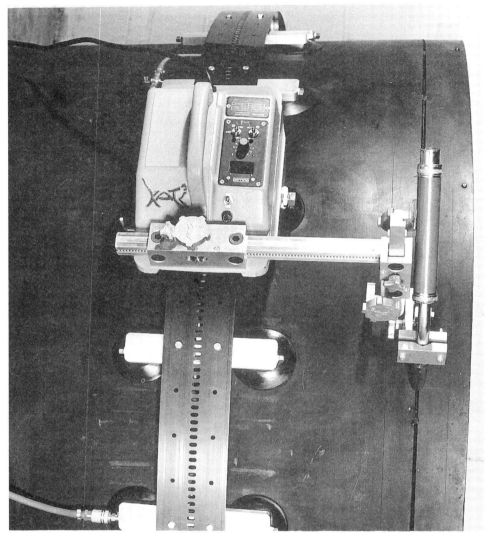

FIG 20 *KAT vacuum track for mounting a MIG welding gun on a self-propelled carriage.*
The wheel system of the carriage 'grips' the track, enabling it to travel along any plant
(Photo: Gullco International Ltd).

FIG 21 Left: *Permanent*
backers.
FIG 22 Right:
Temporary backer.

Control of distortion

Welding distortion is the result of localised heating and cooling. Expansion and
contraction of metal in the weld zone, although constrained by the surrounding

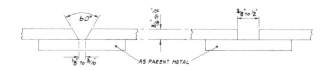

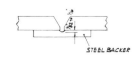

metal, causes both deformation and built-in stresses. Many factors determine how much, and how serious, these problems are, and what should be done to reduce or correct their effects.

The four types of distortion to be found in welded joints are illustrated in Fig 23. They are: angular distortion, longitudinal distortion, shrinkage across the weld, and throat shrinkage. Of these, the last has so little effect that it can be safely ignored.

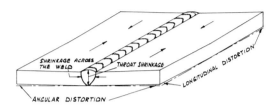 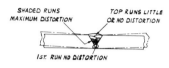

FIG 23 Left: *Types of plate distortion.*
FIG 24 Right: *Single vee'd butt weld.*

ANGULAR DISTORTION

This distortion may be illustrated by a multi-run butt weld (see Fig 26). Provided that the joint is not too rigidly held, the contraction of the first run will merely draw the plates together, without causing distortion. The following runs will tend to cause distortion, as the first run will attempt to resist the contraction of these subsequent runs which, by their combined contraction stresses, create a superior force which tends to lift the edges of the plates in an upward direction. The top runs will have little effect on the amount of distortion caused, as by the time they are deposited the preceding runs are sufficient to provide an anchor against the contraction stresses exerted by the top runs.

In the welding of a single run vee'd butt weld (Fig 24), the resulting distortion will also tend to force the plate edges in an upward direction, as a result of the higher contraction stresses imposed by the larger amount of heated weld metal at the top of the vee.

For welding thicker plates, a double vee'd joint preparation is recommended (see Fig 25). If the runs of welding are deposited in the upper and lower vees alternately, the tendency towards distortion caused by the contraction of the welds in the upper vee is counteracted to a large extent by the opposing counteraction stresses in the lower runs.

The angular distortion described for butt welds is also possible in a fillet welded joint (see Fig 26). As in the case of butt-welded joints, the greater the number of runs employed, the greater could be the distortion. To minimise the effect of angular distortion, the following procedures should be considered and the appropriate action taken: rigid jigging, pre-setting, balancing of stresses by welding from both sides. Where distortion has occurred, straighten mechanically.

LONGITUDINAL DISTORTION

This results from longitudinal contraction of the weld. If there is sufficient trimming allowance, this may not be too troublesome. If contraction of the weld is critical, though, the following could minimise the effect: high welding speeds, back step sequences, multiple weld beads, and rigid jigging. To correct the problem, mechanically stretch the weld area starting from the centre.

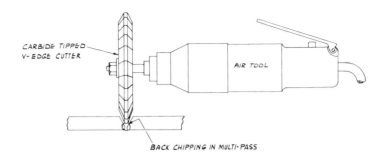

CARBIDE TIPPED
V-EDGE CUTTER

AIR TOOL

BACK CHIPPING IN MULTI-PASS

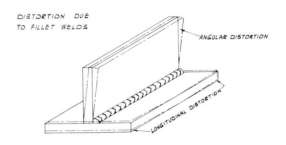

DISTORTION DUE
TO FILLET WELDS

ANGULAR DISTORTION

LONGITUDINAL DISTORTION

FIG 25 Above: *Back chipping in multi-pass welds.*
FIG 26 Below: *Distortion to fillet weld.*

SHRINKAGE ACROSS THE WELD

Shrinkage across the weld is caused by transverse contraction of the weld. To minimise this, use rigid jigging, high welding speeds, and minimum edge preparation.

The following general rules should be considered at the outset to minimise distortion problems:

1 Keep the amount of welding to a minimum. Joints can sometimes be eliminated by using formed or extruded sections. Butt welds should use a minimum of edge preparation and root opening. All weld sizes should be kept as small as strength will allow.

2 Use intermittent welds rather than continuous ones, all other considerations being equal.

3 Use methods and conditions that give the highest welding speeds – eg MIG welding, machine welding, flat position welding.

4 Use jigging where appropriate.

5 Position joints where they will cause least distortion – eg at or near neutral axes, or position them so that weld contraction stresses tend to balance one another.

6 Use a welding sequence that will balance out the stresses.

7 After experimenting to determine the amount, pre-set members, so that when distortion does occur it will result in an acceptable finish.

8 Preheating of the workpiece can help. Best results will be obtained after experimentation.

A simple illustration of distortion is that of two flat plates joined by a single run butt weld. During the process of welding, the free ends of the plate butt will either open out, or close up in front of the weld, unless precautions are taken. If a small electrode, slow speed and low current are employed during welding, there will be, on each side of the joint, a comparatively small heat area expanding and a considerably larger area that is cooling and contracting. The contraction area, therefore, exerts the superior force, and the plates tend to draw together in front of the weld. Conversely, if large gauge electrodes, high welding speed and high currents are used, then there will be a large area of expending metal and a much smaller area of contraction. Thus the expansion area exerts the superior force and the plates will open out in front of the weld as it progresses.

These and other forms of distortion may be kept within reasonable limits by means of wedging, tacking or clamping. If the plates tend to draw together as the weld progresses, the gap may be uniformly maintained by inserting a wedge into the open end and removing it when the welding approaches the end of the joint. When the plates tend to open out in front of the weld, the remedy is simple. By tack welding the plates at intervals along the joint, sufficient restraint is imposed to overcome the gap's tendency to widen. Alternatively, either case may be dealt with by efficiently clamping the joint to prohibit excessive movement of the plates during welding.

Where the avoidance of distortion is of paramount importance, the use of a welding sequence may assist. The two types of sequence most generally employed are the 'stepback' and the 'wandering' sequence, both of which are illustrated in Fig 27. In the stepback sequence, the increments of welding are deposited individually in a direction opposite to that in which the welding is progressing – ie in welding from left to right, each short run of weld metal is deposited working from right to left so that each increment stops where the previous one started.

A wandering sequence is adopted by depositing the first increment at mid

FIG 27 *'Stepback' an*
'wandering' sequenc

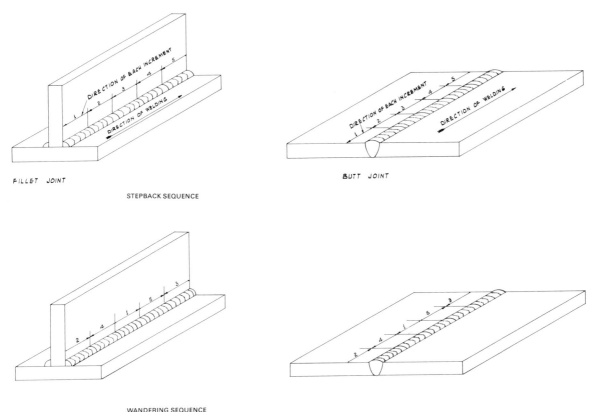

FILLET JOINT

BUTT JOINT

STEPBACK SEQUENCE

WANDERING SEQUENCE

length of the joint, and arranging the succeeding runs in a numbered sequence and a symmetrical pattern on each side of the first. No set order is necessary for these 'staggered' deposits, providing that each increment is always arranged as far as possible from the preceding one.

A good deal of space has been devoted to the subject of distortion, although it is not usually a major problem. (It is less of a problem with the non heat-treatable magnesium-type alloys in the O or M condition, because of their high ductility quality, than with the heat-treatable alloys; and a great deal less of a problem than with steel.) However, if the operator is aware of the internal struggle that is going on within the structure of the metal, then many of the mysteries and frustrations will be more easily understood and counter measures can be put into effect. No hard and fast rules can be laid down about the control of distortion, because there are so many variables that influence the effect. But as the operator gains experience through experiment and practice, he will accumulate the knowledge that will help him to combat and minimise possible problems.

Jigging

FIG 28 *Simple welding jigs.*

Jigs are tools used to locate and hold in position parts that are being worked upon. They can range from a welding tack to a revolving boat jig that allows the whole vessel to be rolled over to any position. The number of times a jig will be used may well determine its complexity.

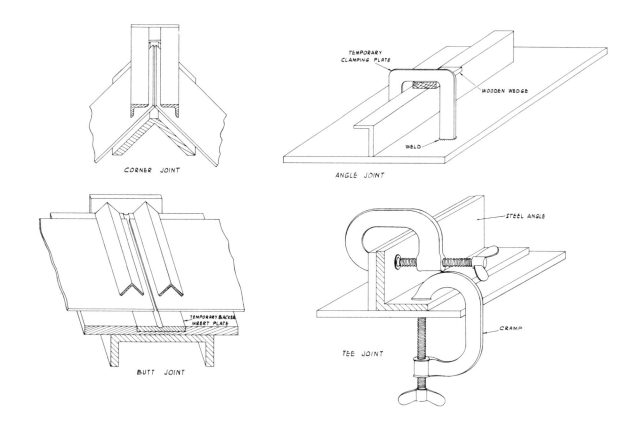

Properly designed jigs provide means for the easy handling of the work and for accurately aligning the edges to be joined, thus giving greater production economy and precision. Jig design should aim at simplicity. Some typical welding jigs are shown in Fig 28.

Weld faults

The tensile strength even of sound welds varies appreciably owing to the effects of joint preparation and method of welding. Not all welds are sound ones, and defects are very often present. The effect these have on weld strength and hence on commercial acceptance is, however, mostly a matter of guesswork. Often welds are rejected simply because the inspection method picks out one particular defect (eg porosity) very well, but with little regard to its influence on both the size and distribution of defects on weld strengths so that acceptance or rejection can be based on realistic standards. There are as yet no published standards whereby to assess the influence of these defects on weld performance. Investigations are being carried out in various laboratories; hopefully, these findings will eventually be published and in time lead to generally accepted standards.

Common defects and their causes

Defects in aluminium welds result principally from faulty welding technique or from bad preparation of joints. These may be dealt with in five groups, each of which can be subdivided. Almost all have an adverse effect on strength, particularly in the area of fatigue.

CRACKING
The most common type of cracking in aluminium welds is longitudinal, occurring along the centre or along the edge of the weld bead. The cause is usually a combination of two factors: susceptibility to hot shortness, and development of restraining stresses. Cracks on the centre of a weld are usually associated with hot shortness in the weld metal, and those at the edge with hot shortness of the parent metal. Both are more likely to occur with a welding technique that produces a large molten weld pool. Hot shortness is purely a function of composition, and to counteract it filler alloys are used that give welds as far removed from the peak cracking composition as possible.

Restraining stresses may be set up by incorrect welding sequences or poor jigging. Both of these can cause cracking. Furthermore, shrinkage of solidifying weld metal under restraint at the end of the weld run may cause crater cracking. This can be avoided by filling the crater with additional metal before the arc is broken or, in automatic welding, by increasing speed and reducing current shortly before the arc is extinguished. Occasionally, crater cracks in a previous pass are not completely repaired by subsequent passes, and the defective areas then have to be chipped out and re-welded. In welding that needs to be fluid-tight, crater cracks are possible sites for leakage.

Weld cracks often undetectable by radiography can result from relative movement between the parent metal surfaces while the weld pool is only partially solidified. Such movement may be caused by spring back, by poor jigging, or by distortion as a result of heat.

Transverse cracking is a comparatively rare defect and only occurs under conditions of longitudinal constraint as are associated with frequent stops and starts or with severe changes in welding speed.

LACK OF FUSION
Lack of fusion is invariably the result either of insufficient current, misalignment, or poor preparation which leaves oxide films or oil on the surfaces to be joined. It can be classified into three readily distinguishable types, illustrated in Fig 29. The first type is lack of penetration, a serious defect resulting from using insufficient current to melt the full joint thickness. In single-pass welds, the bottom (root) surfaces are not melted and a sharp open notch is left. In multipass welds (welded from both sides), the depth of fusion is insufficient to penetrate the opposite weld and an unjoined gap is left in the middle, causing a sharp

FIG 29 *Lack of fusion.*   internal notch.

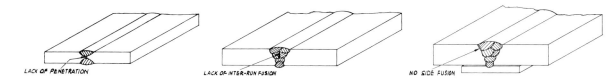

LACK OF PENETRATION   LACK OF INTER-RUN FUSION   NO SIDE FUSION

The second type is lack of inter-run fusion, which occasionally occurs in multi-pass welds. Despite adequate penetration that re-melts the preceding pass, proper interfusion of the succeeding one is prevented by oxide, dirt or oil.

The third type, lack of side fusion, which occurs in TIG welds and in MIG welds in thick plate, is the result of misalignment of the weld torch, insufficient current, or oxide on the parent metal edges, so that the parent metal is only partially fused during welding.

POOR WELD SHAPE
A properly shaped weld provides enough build-up to counteract the lower properties of the cast weld-metal, while at the same time presenting a smooth profile without stress-raising notches. Some common defects in weld shape are illustrated in Fig 31.

Undercutting is reduction in thickness below that of the parent metal; it is caused by misalignment of the torch. The strength of the joint is obviously reduced. Lack of reinforcement, or insufficient build-up of weld metal above the thickness of the parent metal, results in a joint likely to break in the weld.

The effect is similar to that obtained by machining the bead off after welding. The defect can be caused by an unsuitable welding technique or by incorrect edge preparation. Excessive reinforcement also results from choice of an unsuitable technique, while excessive penetration is caused by using too high a welding current, too slow a welding speed, or a badly fitting backing bar. Both these defects, although having little effect on tensile strength, reduce the fatigue strength by increasing the notch effect at the edge of the weld. Excessive penetration can result in 'suck-back' as a result of shrinkage in the root pass, causing in turn a reduction in the area of the weld.

MISALIGNMENT
Poor jigging, and distortion during welding, can lead to welds being made out of

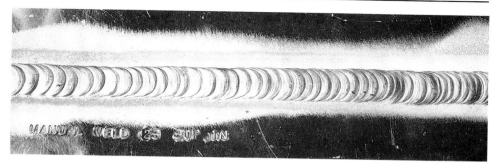

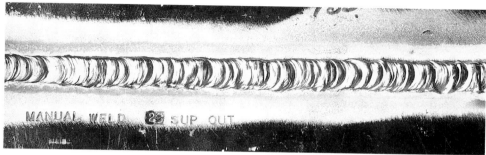

FIG 30 Above: *Good manual TIG weld.* Below: *Inferior manual TIG weld. Poor fusion is caused by a cold weld resulting in much reduced strength* (Photos: Aluminium Laboratories Ltd).

line (Fig 32). There may be no significant loss of static strength in such joints, but the effect on fatigue strength can be serious.

POROSITY

Porosity, common types of which are illustrated in Fig 33, has two main causes. The principal one is the presence of hydrogen, which is readily dissolved in the molten metal and then rejected on solidification. Hydrogen may be picked up from badly prepared welding surfaces, from poor-quality welding wire, or from excessive atmospheric humidity; very occasionally it is present in the parent metal and is released at the weld interface. Another cause of porosity is air that may be trapped by molten weld metal at the base of the joint and forced to rise through the weld. The faster the welding, the more likely it is that air bubbles are trapped. In this respect, TIG welds have an advantage over MIG welds because of the slower rates of cooling involved. Air entrapment may be minimised by attention to joint detail, in allowing for heated air to escape by some means other than via the weld pool. The principal offenders are close-fitting

FIG 31 Left: *Defects in weld shape.*
FIG 32 Right: *Misalignment defects.*

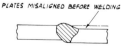

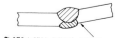
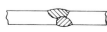

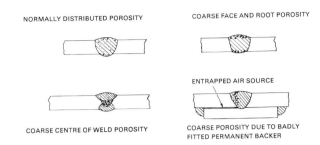

NORMALLY DISTRIBUTED POROSITY   COARSE FACE AND ROOT POROSITY

COARSE CENTRE OF WELD POROSITY

ENTRAPPED AIR SOURCE

COARSE POROSITY DUE TO BADLY
FITTED PERMANENT BACKER

FIG 33 *Porosity.*   joints with permanent backing bars, and square-edge close-butt joints, both of which can give a line of porosity along the centre of the weld.

Linear porosity, in which the pores are concentrated in one plane parallel to the weld line, is nearly always associated with more serious defects such as lack of fusion. Poor gas coverage and dirty parent metal can also result in porosity.

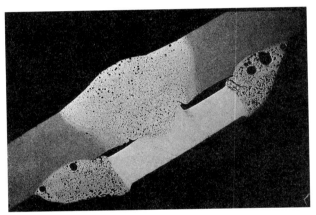
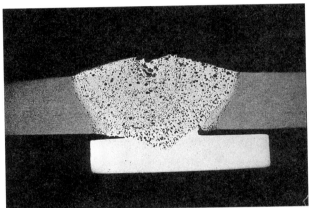

FIG 34 Left: *Enlarged section of a weak joint caused by poor assembly of the permanent backer and excessive porosity, indicating insufficient gas cover.*
Right: *Enlarged section of weak joint caused by poor assembly of the temporary backer and excessive porosity. Had helium been used as the shielding gas, porosity would have been reduced* (Photo: Aluminium Laboratories Ltd).

INCLUSIONS

Oxide and carbon inclusions in aluminium welds may be caused by contamination of the welding surfaces by dirt or oil. Tungsten inclusions result from overheating of the electrode, causing the transfer of molten tungsten across the arc, or from contamination by contact with the weld pool. Copper inclusions can be caused by burn-back resulting in contamination from the contact tube in MIG welding. Tungsten inclusions less than 1.5 mm ($\frac{1}{16}$ in) in diameter are normally considered harmless, but copper inclusions (which dissolve to some extent in aluminium) can cause cracking and thus constitute a serious corrosion hazard. Oxide inclusions in the form of continuous films can seriously reduce strength, but isolated patches have little effect.

INFLUENCE OF DEFECTS ON STATIC STRENGTH

Among defects that have little or no influence on static properties are excess penetration and fine and medium porosity. Coarse porosity has little effect if it is concentrated in the top of the weld bead, but it can reduce tensile strength when concentrated at the centre of the bead. Undercutting and lack of reinforcement can also reduce tensile strength. The efficiency of joints with the bead removed would be to the order of about 85 per cent.

Lack of fusion can have serious effects, especially in cases where sharp open notches result.

INFLUENCE OF DEFECTS ON FATIGUE STRENGTH
The fatigue behaviour of butt welds depends principally on the shape of the reinforcement and on whether or not the reinforcement is removed. In the as-welded condition, fatigue failure normally occurs at the edge of the bead, because of the stress-raising effect of the change in cross-section at this point. Bead shape is thus of primary importance, and imperfections inside the weld are less significant. When the bead is removed, however, flaws in the cast metal weld itself have greater significance, with failure sometimes occurring through the weld.

Misalignments in butt joints increase the general stress level and can reduce the fatigue strength many times.

Inspection and testing

Inspection and testing of welded joints is necessary to obtain and maintain the required joint quality in production. The standards to which welds are inspected will vary according to the ultimate use of the weld in question. The methods recommended here are representative of good commercial practice. They may be classified under two general headings: non-destructive testing, and destructive testing.

NON-DESTRUCTIVE TESTING
This is usually carried out by three methods of examination: visual, dye penetrant, and radiography.

Visual examination, particularly with the aid of a magnifying lens, will readily indicate such defects as non-uniform appearance, incomplete penetration on welds made from one side, surface cracks, undercut and overhang. Non-uniformity is not in itself a defect, but a non-uniform weld bead may well indicate the weld was not properly made, and more serious defects may be present.

Dye penetrant may be used to locate surface cracks, surface porosity, and incomplete fusion where this extends to the surface of a weld. There are several proprietary bands of dye penetrant available, and all have their special instructions for use. The general principles are:

1 Clean and degrease the area.
2 Apply the dye penetrant; this finds its way into extremely small surface openings.
3 Remove the excess surface penetrant with special penetrant remover.
4 Spray the area with a fine film of developer. The surface weld defects show up in a very distinctive colour.

The use of dye penetrants is not recommended by many authorities because of the difficulty of adequately cleaning the contaminated area before a repair can be attempted. Used sparingly and with a full appreciation of the problem, they can be a quick and cheap aid.

Radiography provides a permanent record of the interior condition of the weld. It is usual to X-ray butt welds only. The equipment is relatively expensive, and trained personnel are required to operate it and interpret the resulting film.

DESTRUCTIVE TESTING

This can be classified under three main headings: fracture testing, bend testing, and tensile testing.

Fracture testing is an effective and economical method of generally testing fillet and butt welds. In the case of fillet welds, one side only should be welded, and the test piece secured in a vice with the weld uppermost. The upright plate is then forced up over the weld either by adjustable spanner or hammer. A good weld should bend almost flat before breaking. Lack of fusion will be clearly shown. For testing butt welds, the nick-break is used. For this the specimen weld reinforcement and ends are notched with a saw cut, placed in a vice, and the free end hammered very sharply. Examination will reveal such defects as porosity, inclusions, lack of penetration, lack of fusion, and underbead cracking (see Fig 35).

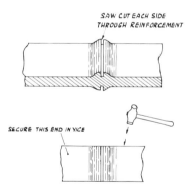

FIG 35 *Nick-break test.*

Bend testing is used on butt welds. The specimen should be cleaned of weld bead and reinforcement, and bent through 180°, around a radius of about 3 T (3 × thickness of material). This test can be performed on a fly press or modified pipe bending machine.

Tensile testing is carried out on a special machine to determine tensile strength, yield strength and elongation. The two sides of the welded joint are secured in the machine and the specimen pulled apart. Classification societies often call for this test to be carried out.

Safety precautions

It goes without saying that any complex piece of electrical equipment such as a welding machine should only be operated by trained personnel – or trainees under the direction of trained personnel. Modifications to the machine, and fault finding within it, must be carried out by those qualified to do so. Many machines are fitted with elaborate safety devices that are not necessarily essential to the working of the machine, but if the machine is operated without them both the machine and the operator could be at risk.

There should be adequate ventilation in the welding area to remove the fumes created by the process. Although these fumes are relatively harmless, they can make working in a confined space very unpleasant. It is recommended that personnel working in an area where fumes are concentrated should drink an extra pint of milk each day. This also applies to places where paint spraying is carried out.

Exposure of the skin to the rays of a welding arc, even for a short time, can result in a condition similar to sunburn. It is important, therefore, that the operator should protect all exposed areas of skin, particularly of the hands, head and back of the neck. Substantial dark clothing should be worn to reduce reflection. Soft leather gauntlet gloves should be worn to protect the hands and arms. Helmets with recommended dark lens and lens protection should be worn. Where spatter is encountered, a leather apron should be worn in addition to other protective clothing. Wherever possible, screens should surround the welding area to protect other workers from accidental sight of the welding arc. When this does occur, it can cause great pain behind the eyes. Special eye drops are available for this condition and, if applied promptly, can prevent or greatly reduce any suffering.

At least one qualified person should always be on the premises to render first aid, with a laid-down procedure for dealing with more serious cases. Fire hazards should also be adequately provided for.

5 • FASTENINGS

Rivets

Of all the mechanical methods of fastening, rivets are probably the most widely used. There are two general types of rivets: blind, fitted from one side only; and solid, fitted from one side with points burred over on the other side.

BLIND RIVETS

These are supplied in various metals – steel, stainless steel, copper, monel and aluminium alloy – and with countersunk or domed heads. The shank of the rivet is entered from the outside of the workpiece. A mandrel, usually steel, protrudes from the head and is gripped in the jaws of a special tool; the jaws pull the mandrel and, in so doing, they bunch up the rivet on the inside and break off the mandrel at a predetermined load. The advantages are that only one operator is involved, the work can be done from one side only, and that as the rivet is squeezed tight instead of hammered, a curved workpiece would not tend to straighten (as it does under continued hammering). Depending on the application, the rivets are supplied as 'open' or 'sealed'. In the open rivet the mandrel is pulled right through the rivet, leaving a hollow centre. These are, of course, used only on non-watertight joints, interior trim, etc. The sealed type are supplied with a short break, or long break mandrel, and the interior is completely blanked off. In the short break, the mandrel breaks off well inside the rivet (see Fig 36); in the long break, the mandrel breaks off at the head of the rivet and is in fact exposed. The short break has the advantage of the mandrel breaking inside the rivet, leaving a smooth head, and when painted over this seals the steel mandrel inside from 'bleeding' through the paint scheme. The steel mandrel on the long break extends just through the head and leaves a sharp edge. For appearance and safety, this has to be ground smooth.

When painted over, there is more chance of this 'bleeding' through the paint scheme. Both types of watertight rivet have the same tensile strength, but the long break has almost twice the shear strength as the short break. For all normal applications, the strength of the short break is sufficient. Only when very high shear loads are applied is the long break necessary. The most popular diameters are 3 mm ($\frac{1}{8}$ in) for interior, and 4.6 mm ($\frac{3}{16}$ in) for exterior applications such as superstructures etc. The length of the rivet is governed by the plate thickness to be joined, sometimes called the 'grip thickness'. Tables are available from the manufacturers that detail the code by which the rivets are ordered. They also recommend the hole sizes to be bored to receive the rivet.

SOLID RIVETS

As the name implies, this rivet is formed from solid bar. The manufactured head can be snap, pan, or countersunk. The points (the end that is hammered over) are usually snap or countersunk. The rivet is entered from one side of the work-

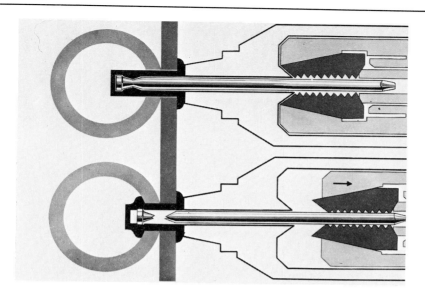

piece, a 'dolly' or heavy weight is held to the head, and the point is hammered or burred over, usually with a pneumatic reciprocating gun fitted with a snap. The size of snap is determined by the diameter of the rivet. The hammering over can be done by hand in the smaller diameters, but is not recommended for the larger rivets, because of the work hardening effect of the hammering (ie becoming brittle when worked). A few heavy blows applied quickly tend to provide a tighter joint. A good general formula for the rivet length is: $L - 1.10 \times$ grip thickness $+ 1.15 \times$ diameter of rivet. Solid rivets can be obtained in diameters from 1.5 mm ($\frac{1}{16}$ in) to 9 mm ($\frac{3}{8}$ in) in increments of 0.75 mm ($\frac{1}{32}$ in).

The choice of blind or solid rivets will depend chiefly on cost, appearance, availability, and whether both sides of the workpiece are accessible. Some operators consider there is more control over the amount the solid rivet can be drawn up. The solid rivet is cheaper, but the operation is much noisier.

The material for the rivet should be as similar to the parent metal as is available. If the parent metal is NS 8 aluminium alloy, normally the closest rivet material is NE 6 and this is quite compatible.

Where a watertight joint is required, the faying or mating surfaces, and the rivet shank, should be wet assembled with a suitable elastomer. Berger Chemicals produce an excellent one known as PRC Rubber Calk 150, and it is a two-part polysulphide rubber. Both mating surfaces should be degreased and lightly

FIG 36 *'Pop' sealed-type rivet setting sequence.*

FIG 37 *Riveted joints.*

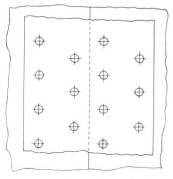

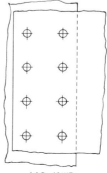

BUTT STRAP REELED SPACING   BUTT STRAP CHAIN SPACING   LAP JOINT

coated immediately prior to joining. The mixture usually has a limited life when mixed, so only the minimum quantity should be mixed at a time.

The simplest form of riveted joints is the lap joint, which may have one, two, three or four rows of rivets. Butt straps are also used, with either single or double rows of rivets (see Fig 37).

When building to classification society rules, their rule book gives the diameter, pitch, spacing between rows, and distance of rivets from the plate edge for each piece of structure. For Admiralty work, pitch is normally given as:

Maximum: $4\frac{1}{2}$ diameters in oiltight work
  5 diameters in watertight work
  8 diameters otherwise

Clear distance from edge of plate, one diameter $+3\,\mathrm{mm}$ ($\frac{1}{8}$ in).

Bolts and other fastenings

Depending on the location and strength requirements, bolts will normally be galvanised mild steel or stainless steel. Above the waterline, or for internal structure, where a strength requirement not exceeding about 28 tons per sq in UTS is sufficient, galvanised mild steel would be suitable. Zinc plating will not protect mild steel against seawater indefinitely, however, so painting with etch primer plus a full paint scheme is recommended.

Below the waterline, or where the strength factor demands are greater, stainless steel should be used. Where the risk of corrosion is greatest – ie immersed in salt water – 18/8 austenitic stainless steel cadmium plated bolts would considerably reduce galvanic corrosion.

All bimetal joints and all joints of wood to metal should be met assembled with a suitable jointing compound. Nuts should, wherever possible, be of a similar material to the bolts they secure. Cadmium plated steel nuts, on cadmium plated stainless steel bolts, is sometimes an acceptable compromise – though not ideal. Various types of locknuts are available; among the more usual ones are:

- The 'slipnot', a self-locking nut, embodying a collet-like frictional metallic grip.
- The 'slitnot'; this has an axially stretched neck.
- The 'nylock', with a nylon insert; the nylon initially has a plain bore, but when the nut is screwed tight, a thread is cut into the nylon and grips very tightly around the bolt.

These newer types of locknuts are tending to supersede the older second locknut, spring washers, and castle nuts with split pins.

It is sometimes very useful to attach a temporary or permanent thread to the workpiece. This can, of course, be done by tapping a thread if the parent metal is thick enough. Putting a thread into aluminium has limitations, though, because of the softness of aluminium and its alloys. The danger exists of stripping the thread, so more threads than normal are required. It is quite usual for tapped aluminium bosses to be welded to aluminium tanks, to receive valves, etc. A word of warning here though. An aluminium shank must never be screwed into an aluminium tapped hole. Even before a couple of threads had been entered, the whole thing would grind together and be very difficult to part.

Where it is necessary to provide a deep tapped hole in thin sheet metal, hank

FIG 38 Above: *The 7.6 m (25 ft), 40 knot yacht tender* Khalid *built for Adnan Khashoggi, designed by Shead Design.*

Right: Khalid *in frame. Note the extra frames and stringers to accommodate impact at high speed.*
Below left: Khalid's *transom cutouts are for mounting zed drives. The deep-vee bottom prevents excessive slamming.*
Below right: Khalid's *5 mm ($\frac{1}{5}$ in) welded bottom and 1.5 mm ($\frac{1}{16}$ in) riveted topsides. Integral swages on the topsides provide extra stiffening without extra weight.*

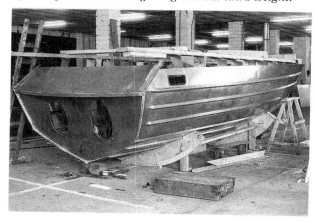

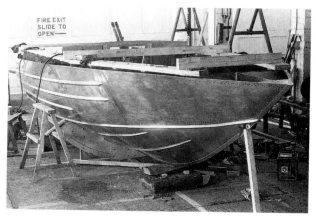

rivet bushes are often used. These are produced by several manufacturers and in various threads and sizes. Where there is a need for watertightness, a blank end can be supplied. The hank bush is essentially a nut, with a collar, that is entered into a hole in the workpiece and riveted over (see Fig 39).

Anchor nuts are also extensively used. These consist of a captive nut retained in a cage, and this in turn is riveted to the workpiece. The nuts can be either fixed or floating to provide greater flexibility in lining up. There are many other types of captive nut for specialist applications.

Another very useful method of attaching a thread is with a 'Heli-Coil'. This is a stainless steel screw thread insert. A hole is drilled in the workpiece and is then

FIG 39 Left: *Hank bush*.
FIG 40 Right: *'Dzus' fastener*.

tapped with special 'Heli-Coil' tap. The stainless steel insert is then wound into the tapped hole with a special inserting tool. Where the thickness of metal is sufficient and the bolt needs to be tightened hard, these inserts are very popular. They are quick to install, relatively inexpensive, and can be worked from one side only. They will not work loose, but can be extracted with a special tool.

Another way of keeping a panel in position is with a 'Dzus' fastener. This consists of a receptacle riveted to the parent metal, and a bolt held captive in the panel. The bolt is screwed into the receptacle with a special coarse quick action thread, and is retained in the panel with a grommet (see Fig 40).

Self-tapping screws are sometimes used in thin panels, but the thread in the aluminium tends to strip after a few tightenings.

Adhesives

Where adhesive bonding is used for attaching insulation and trim on boats, the rubber-base compounds are often used. Resin-type coatings are also suitable where curing takes place at room temperature and simple fixing jigs can be employed.

For making structural joints between aluminium surfaces, several high strength adhesives are available. Some of these require curing by tightly controlled applications of heat and mating pressures. This calls for special ovens and complex fixing jigs. Only considerable volume throughput would justify the initial capital investment.

Adhesives are not widely used in small-scale production of aluminium boats. This may be because of traditional conservatism or lack of knowledge. There is need for experimentation in choice of adhesive, design of joint, and technique of application. It is highly likely that adhesives will figure more prominently in the joining of aluminium in the future. (See Chapter 21 Racing Powerboats.)

6 ◆ LINES AND LAYING OFF

It is not my intention here to describe in great detail the way in which a set of lines is assembled by the designer and laid off by the loftsman. These basic principles appear in so many publications that repetition is unwarranted. For the uninitiated, though, a very brief outline is set out below.

Lines plans are the traditional graphic method by which a designer indicates to the builder, in three-dimensional form, the shape that a vessel will take. Three views are needed: profile or sheer, half breadth or plan view, and body plan or half sections. It is necessary to draw all views to full size, for it is only when the lines pass through the same points in each view, all fair, can we be certain that the individual plates will present a continuous and pleasing curve when the plating has been fitted. A table of offsets is provided to enable the basic lines to be drawn. These offsets, ie dimensions measured from particular datum lines, are taken about station lines. These station lines are positioned solely for the convenience of the designer; the reason we have to duplicate full size what he has already provided us with on a small scale, is simply to check his accuracy.

Sometimes, when working to the dimensions given, or offsets, the lines will not fair in all three views. It is the loftsman's job to ensure that all the views do fair and, where necessary, to correct the offsets. A typical lines plan is shown in Fig 41.

With the buttock lines faired in the profile and the waterlines faired in the half breadth, verticals are raised at all bulkhead and frame stations. From these two views, a new body plan can be drawn that indicates half sections at all these new station positions. We can now produce templates to indicate the outline of all frames and bulkheads. Only half the section need be produced, because we can turn the template over and work about the centreline.

Longitudinal or fore and aft members such as stem and keel, engine beds, stringers, spray rails, chines, gunwales, etc can now be drawn in and templates made as necessary.

Templates are best produced from solid material such as sheets of ply or hardboard. If produced from framed material such as slats of wood around the perimeter, with struts holding them together, there is a high risk of distortion. The templates are used to mark the outline of the section on to the aluminium sheets. The sheets or extrusions are then tacked together and checked with the templates. Where distortion has occurred, it must be corrected, and then finally welded.

When very large sheets are used for the skin, or where a lot of shape is encountered, it is sometimes necessary, or at least very convenient, to predetermine the final shape of the hull plating. One method by which this is achieved is by triangulation. This enables us to develop a curved surface on to a flat plane. On a chine boat this is often only considered necessary in the fore part of the bottom, although of course it can be used on any part of the hull. The surface is

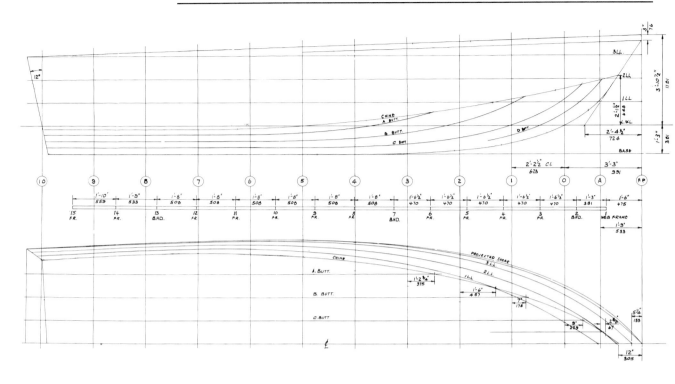

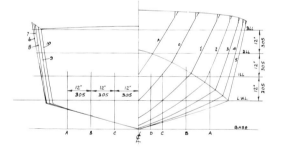

TABLE OF OFFSETS

NUMBER OF STATIONS	A	O	1	2	3	4	5	6	7	8	9	10	
HEIGHTS ABOVE BASE													
PROJECTED SHEER	STRAIGHT LINE F.P TO STN. 10											4-3-2 / 1301	INCHES / m.m
BUTTOCK C	3-1-2 / 946	2-4-4 / 724	1-3-2 / 387	0-8-4 / 216	0-5-3 / 137	0-4-0 / 102	0-3-4 / 89	STRAIGHT LINE				0-3-4 / 89	INCHES / m.m
BUTTOCK B	—	—	2-2-1 / 667	1-4-4 / 419	0-11-2 / 286	0-8-4 / 216	0-7-1 / 181	0-6-7 / 165	STRAIGHT LINE			0-6-7 / 165	INCHES / m.m
BUTTOCK A	—	—	—	—	1-6-4 / 470	1-1-6 / 349	0-8-2 / 286	0-10-3 / 264	STRAIGHT LINE			0-10-3 / 264	INCHES / m.m
CHINE	3-2-2 / 972	2-10-0 / 864	2-4-4 / 724	1-11-7 / 606	1-8-0 / 508	1-5-1 / 435	1-3-0 / 381	1-1-4 / 343	1-1-0 / 330	STRAIGHT LINE		1-1-0 / 330	INCHES / m.m
KEEL	2-4-0 / 711	1-3-0 / 381	0-5-7 / 149	0-2-0 / 51	0-0-3 / 10	—	—	—	—	—	—	—	INCHES / m.m
HALF BREADTHS													
PROJECTED SHEER	1-7-4 / 495	2-6-0 / 762	3-4-4 / 1029	3-10-6 / 1177	4-2-5 / 1286	4-4-5 / 1337	4-5-6 / 1365	4-5-5 / 1362	4-4-7 / 1343	4-4-7 / 1321	4-2-6 / 1289	4-1-2 / 1251	
3 L.L.	1-1-6 / 349	2-1-1 / 638	3-0-6 / 933	3-8-1 / 1121	4-0-6 / 1238	4-4-7 / 1308	4-5-0 / 1343	4-4-3 / 1346	4-3-5 / 1330	4-2-3 / 1311	4-1-1 / 1280	1248	
2 L.L.	0-7-0 / 178	1-6-7 / 479	2-7-2 / 784	3-3-4 / 1003	3-9-1 / 1146	4-0-3 / 1223	4-2-3 / 1280	4-3-1 / 1299	4-2-7 / 1292	4-2-0 / 1270	4-0-6 / 1238	3-11-3 / 1203	
1 L.L.	—	2-10-5 / 879	3-5-0 / 1041	3-9-2 / 1149	3-11-5 / 1210	4-1-1 / 1245	4-1-0 / 1245	4-0-1 / 1222	3-10-7 / 1181	3-9-3 / 1153			
CHINE	0-6-5 / 168	1-4-3 / 416	2-2-2 / 667	2-9-3 / 848	3-2-5 / 981	3-6-4 / 1080	3-9-0 / 1143	3-10-2 / 1175	3-10-6 / 1187	3-10-1 / 1172	3-8-6 / 1137	3-7-0 / 1092	

DIMENSIONS IN FEET INCHES & EIGHTHS OF AN INCH & MILLIMETRS TO INSIDE OF SKIN

PRINCIPAL DIMENSIONS

LENGTH OVERALL _____ 26'-0"
MOULDED BEAM MAX. _____ 8'-11½"
MOULDED CHINE BEAM MAX. _____ 7'-9½"
MOULDED DEPTH _____ 4'-7¾"

FIG 41 *Typical lines plan.*

divided up into a number of adjoining triangles, as was shown in Fig 5. By drawing diagonal lines from chine to keel, the surface is triangulated for development (see Fig 42). To lay out or develop the hull surface, the true lengths of all sides of all triangles must be determined. This is accomplished by the use of right triangles. The length of one side of these triangles as they appear in the plan is used for the base, and their differences in elevation, as they appear in the profile, is used for the vertical height. By laying out these two lines at right angles to one another, the length of the hypotenuse, which is the true length, is deter-

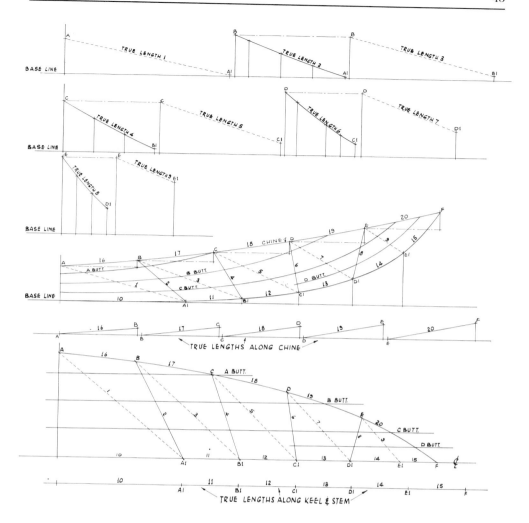

FIG 42 *Development of true lengths for triangulation.*

mined. The true lengths are now used as radii of arcs which are intersected to form the final flat expansion. The diagonals that are curved are determined from the buttock intersections much in the same way as the frames. Their true lengths are determined by girthing the curve. By building up the triangles in a continuous line, the final shape of the sheet is determined (see Fig 43).

Where a curved transom is required, it is necessary to produce an expanded view – ie when the transom is unwrapped, so that it can be cut out of flat plates, and when shaped, the periphery will line up with the extension of the plating. There are several ways of developing or producing an expanded view of the transom. A fairly straightforward way is illustrated in Fig 44. This indicates the profile and plan view of the aft section of a vessel with a rounded transom.

The radius is shown in the plan view with the centreline of the arc struck from the centreline of the boat. Also shown in both views are three buttock lines – A, B and C – and three waterlines – 1, 2 and 3. To obtain the expanded view of the transom, all that is necessary is to unwrap the transom by flattening it out. At the same time, flatten out the waterlines and buttocks and, by measuring these round the shaped transom with a batten, straighten out the batten. By transfer-ring and projecting these new marks on to our expanded view and obtaining a

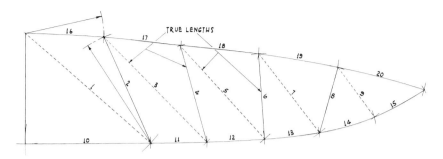

FIG 43 *Expansion of forward bottom plate by triangulation.*

series of spots on our newly drawn waterlines and buttocks, these indicate the extremities of the expanded transom. The periphery of the transom is completed by joining these spots with a fair line.

Let's take this a step at a time. On the profile, continue the waterlines normal to the rake or slope of the transom. Lay a batten around the curve of the transom and on it mark the position of the buttock lines. Straighten out the batten, and mark in these expanded buttock lines. We now have a grid of expanded buttocks and waterlines laying normal to the slope of the transom. By projecting the termination of the buttock lines in the profile to obtain the heights, and measuring round the curved waterlines in the plan view to obtain the half breadths, then straightening out the batten and transferring these spots on the relative waterlines in the expanded view and, as already indicated, by joining these spots with a fair line, we have the expanded view of the transom.

FIG 44 *Development of expanded transom.*

Where there is a lot of shape in the hull, as for some round bilge boats, it may

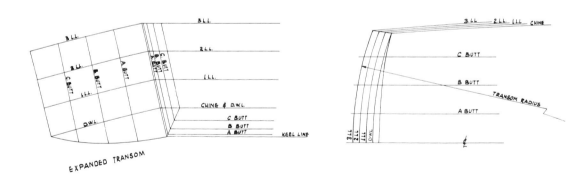

be necessary to draw in extra buttocks or waterlines to obtain extra spots; this enables a more accurate curve to be drawn.

Laying off demands a high degree of accuracy in measuring and marking. Any inaccuracies must be resolved in the three views. If they are not, problems will inevitably arise when fairing in the hull.

The scrieve board – ie the area where the lines are laid down – must be flat and kept free of all traffic. A set of lines accurately and well set out, if preserved, can be of great value throughout the entire building period of the vessel. It is often very time saving to have the opportunity to refer back to the full-size lines for a multitude of dimensional requirements, particularly in connection with sterngear.

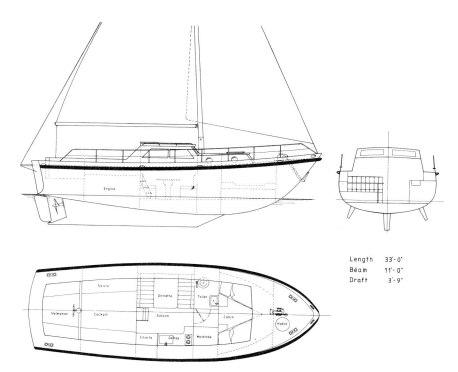

Length   33'- 0"
Beam   11'- 0"
Draft   3'- 9"

FIG 45 *Arrangement of accommodation for motor sailer* Delos.

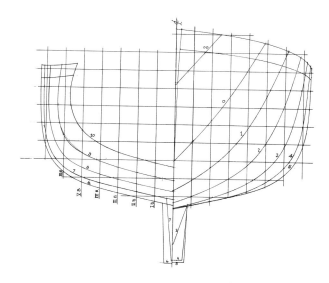

FIG 46(a) *Lines plan for motor sailer* Delos. *See also following pages.*

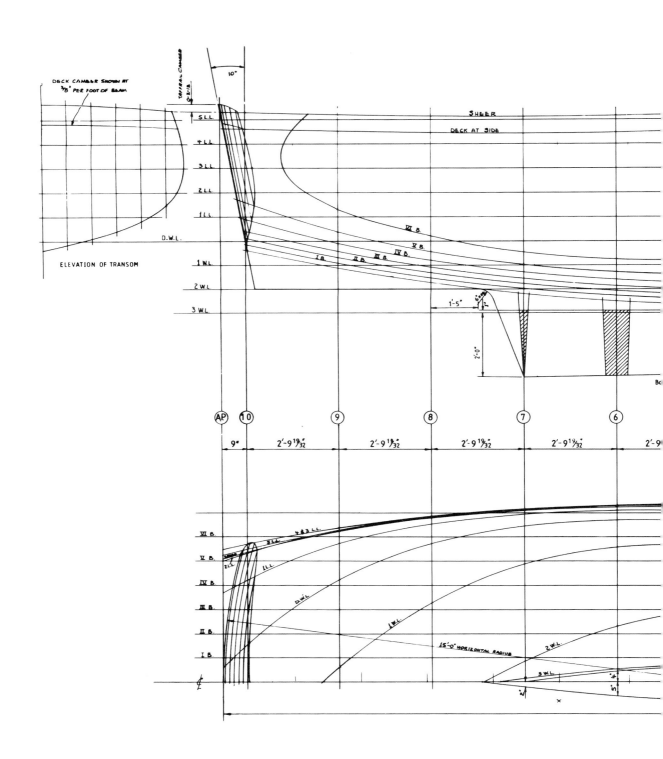

FIG 46(b) *Lines plan for motor sailer* Delos.

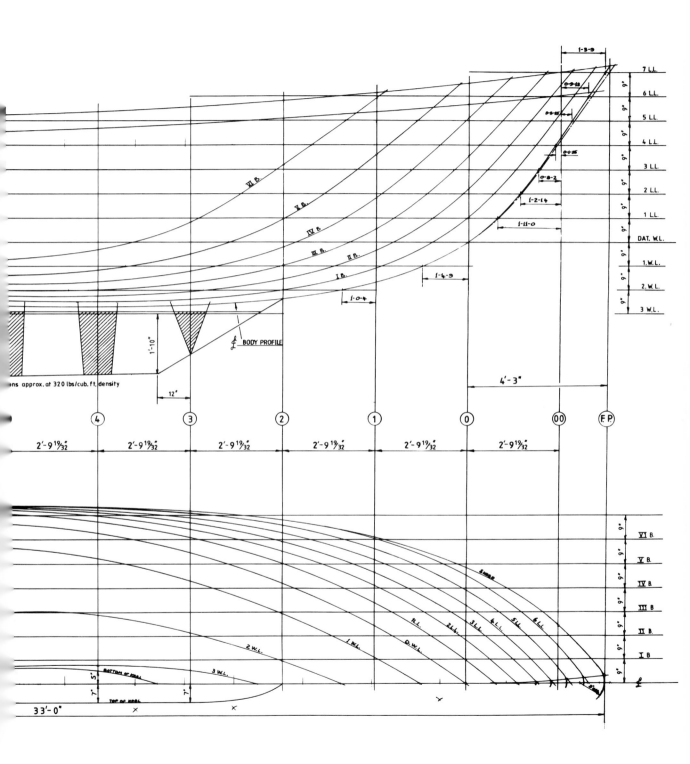

7 LL.

6 LL.

5 LL.

4 LL.

3 LL.

2 LL.

1 LL.

DAT. W.L.

1.W.L.

2. W.L.

3 W.L.

1-3-9

0-9-13

0-9-13

0-1-15

0-8-2

1-2-14

1-11-0

VI B.

V B.

IV B.

III B.

II B.

I B.

1-4-9

1-0-4

℄ BODY PROFILE

1'-10"

12"

4'-3"

9"

9"

9"

9"

9"

9"

9"

9"

...ns approx. at 320 lbs/cub. ft. density

④   ③   ②   ①   ⓪   ⓪⓪   F.P.

2'-9¹⁹/₃₂"   2'-9¹⁹/₃₂"   2'-9¹⁹/₃₂"   2'-9¹⁹/₃₂"   2'-9¹⁹/₃₂"   2'-9¹⁹/₃₂"

VI B.

V B.

IV B.

III B.

II B.

I B.

6 W.R.

R.L.

2 L.L.

3 L.L.

4 L.L.

5 L.L.

6 L.L.

1 W.L.

D.W.L.

2 W.L.

3 W.L.

S WR.R.

BOTTOM OF KEEL

5"

7"

7"

TOP OF KEEL

33'-0"

9"

9"

9"

9"

9"

9"

9"

℄

7 ◆ Jigs

The amount of jig making will to some extent depend on the number of craft to be built to the same design, or the number of precisely similar parts to a craft. Jigs can be broadly divided into two classes: the essential jigs that have to be produced in order to build the craft, and the convenience jigs that are produced in order to save time where quantity production is involved.

The building jig is the largest and most important one. It ranges from simple building blocks to a master assembly-welding fixture, which is supported at each end by trunnion swivel mountings that can be rotated to bring any desired portion of the hull to the top. One company in the United States produces a 4.2 m (14 ft) runabout on such a jig where gunwales, stem, keel and chine extrusions are clamped in position, after which the hull plating is fitted and clamped in place. A series of pneumatic holding clamps, actuated from a control console, pulls the sheets and extrusions together to produce the proper welding gap. Circuit lights indicate when each hull section is properly positioned, and an automatically guided welding gun runs on a roller track. The welding head is

FIG 47 *A 41 m (134 ft) monohull fast passenger vessel. The large hull is erected in the upright stance* (Photo: FBM Marine Ltd).

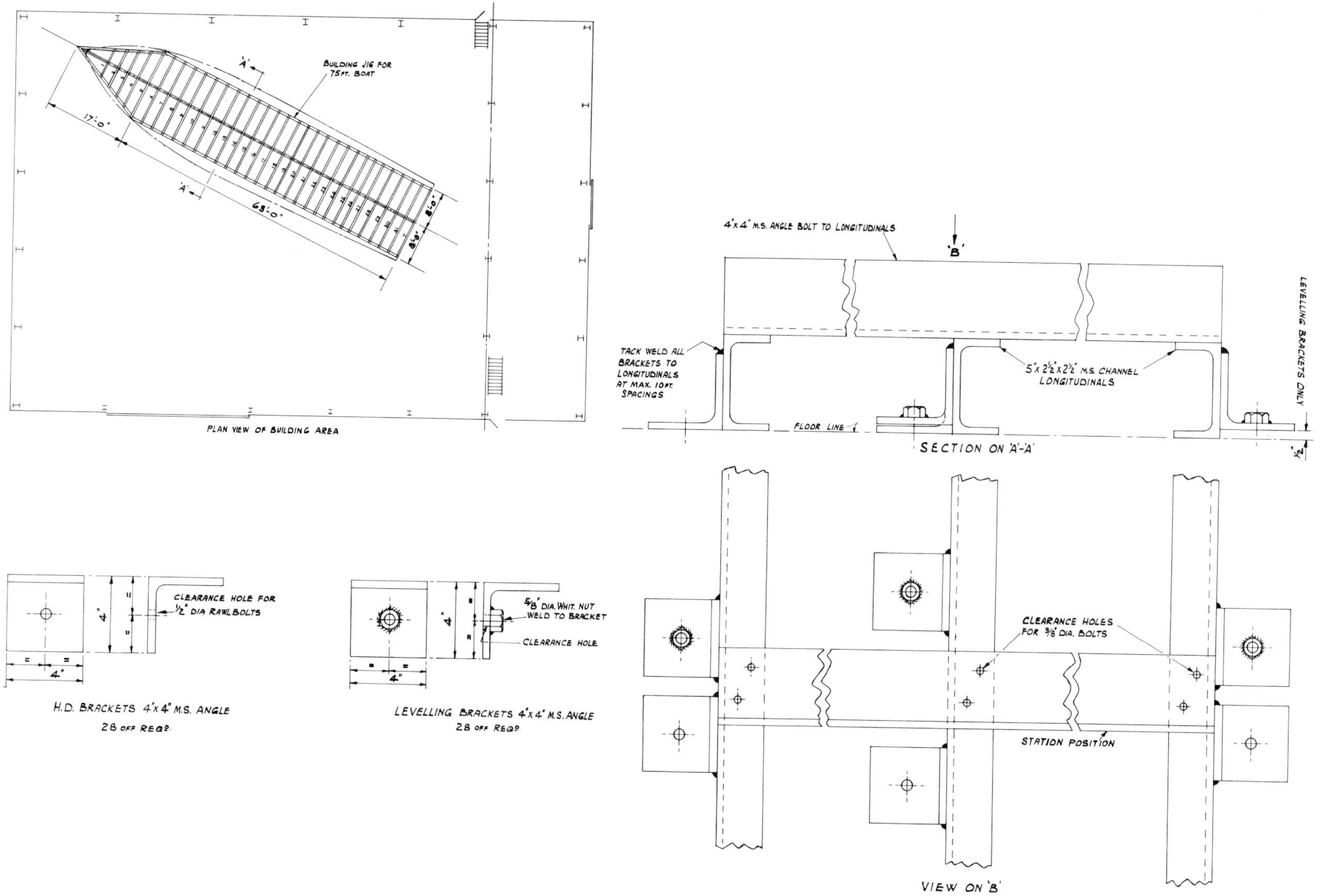

LEVELLING BRACKETS ONLY

4" x 4" M.S. ANGLE BOLT TO LONGITUDINALS

5" x 2½" x 2½" M.S. CHANNEL LONGITUDINALS

SECTION ON 'A'-'A'

FLOOR LINE

TACK WELD ALL BRACKETS TO LONGITUDINALS AT MAX. 10ft SPACINGS

CLEARANCE HOLES FOR ⅝" DIA. BOLTS

STATION POSITION

VIEW ON 'B'

⅝" DIA. WHIT NUT WELD TO BRACKET

CLEARANCE HOLE

LEVELLING BRACKETS 4" x 4" M.S. ANGLE
28 OFF REQ?

CLEARANCE HOLE FOR ½" DIA RAWLBOLTS

H.D. BRACKETS 4" x 4" M.S. ANGLE
28 OFF REQ?

BUILDING JIG FOR 75ft. BOAT

68'-0"

17'-0"

PLAN VIEW OF BUILDING AREA

FIG 48 *Building a jig for a 22.8m (75ft) chine boat.*

FIG 49   *Jig with bulkheads set up.*

FIG 50   *Wooden former for curved transom.*

suspended and can be raised or lowered automatically, as well as moved
longitudinally during welding.

A set of timing circuits, all connected to the control console, means the welding operation is largely automatic. Only two people are required: the console
operator and a man to place the aluminium sheets and extrusions on the frame.
Circulating water is run to the welding gun and also to the chill bars which are
permanent elements of the welding fixture, and are located to bear against the
hull plates where welding heat input is concentrated. Seam welding with this
equipment proceeds at the rate of about 1.2 m (4 ft) per minute.

There are many variations of jigs, from the most simple to the sophisticated
one described above. The determining factor is: over how many craft can the
cost of the jig be amortised? There can be no doubt that, given the correct set up,
the labour costs of producing an aluminium hull can be as cheap, or cheaper, as
any other form of construction.

A typical simple building jig is illustrated in Fig 48. This is for a 22.8 m (75 ft)
chine boat. Fig 49 shows the jig constructed and the forward bulkheads being set
up. The jig consists essentially of two steel channel sections that follow very
broadly the outline of the sheer in plan form, with a similar channel on the
centreline. There are steel angles bolted to these three channels, with the
upright outside face directly positioned on each bulkhead and frame station.
The whole jig is levelled by means of the jacking screws, and bolted to the
concrete floor – using distance pieces under the securing lugs as necessary. We

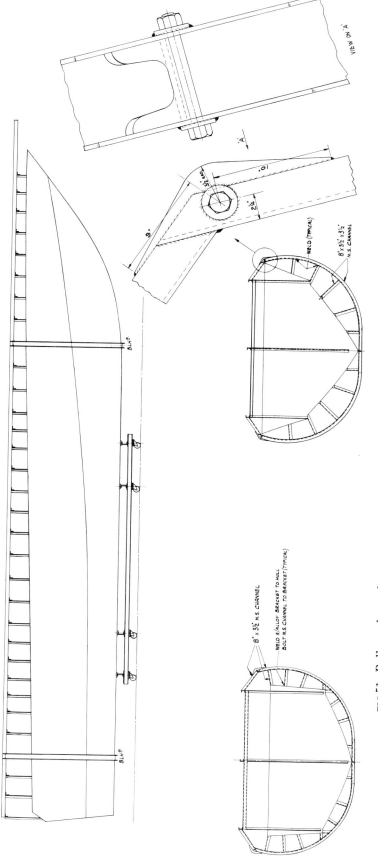

VIEW ON 'A'

WELD (TYPICAL)

8" x 3½" x 3½"
M.S. CHANNEL

8" x 3½" M.S. CHANNEL

WELD R/ALLOY BRACKET TO HULL

BOLT M.S. CHANNEL TO BRACKET (TYPICAL)

BLH⁰

BLH⁰

FIG 51 *Roll over hoops for a 22.8m (75 ft) boat.*

now have a datum face and centreline to work to. The bulkheads and frames are set up on light gauge steel angles and braced together.

When the hull has been completed and is ready for turning over, the jig is left in position and hull and jig are turned as one unit. The jig gives rigidity to the hull and prevents any possibility of distortion during the turning operation.

Where a curved transom is required, a wooden former such as that shown in Fig 50 is easy to construct. The face of the wooden former should be concave, so that after forming by the rollers the transom plates are laid and secured temporarily to the wooden framing. The aluminium stiffeners are then shaped and positioned and the welding is completed.

Where unit construction is used – ie whole parts are sub-assembled – very precise and substantial jigs are needed so that mating parts will match. This type of construction, though more expensive on jigging, does enable more operators to be employed at the same time and can considerably reduce the overall building time, and occupancy, of the building berth.

The building jigs so far described have been on the assumption of building upside down. The advantages of this so outweigh the disadvantages (provided there is enough room and equipment to execute the turnover) that it is difficult to conceive of building upright from choice. Some of the advantages are as follows:

- All the frame work and strutting can be contained within the perimeters of the hull.
- Once the hull plates have been lifted into approximate position, then gravity holds them there.
- Welding is to a very large extent all downhand, and this alone makes it worthwhile.
- Temporary strutting of plates in position is eliminated.
- Plates can be finally positioned with greater accuracy.
- More plates can be welded together off the job because of the easier assembly.
- It is considerably easier to position and true up the bulkheads and frames.
- The stemhead can be secured to a substantial base.
- Because the jig is heavy and rigid there is far less chance of serious welding distortion.
- From the safety angle, there is less likelihood of cramps becoming loose and plates falling.

The big *disadvantage* is that the vessel has to be turned. This can be accomplished by one of two methods: turning in situ by means of a revolving jig, or rolling over on hoops secured to the hull after completion.

The revolving jig has the advantage of requiring less turning space, but is probably restricted to smaller vessels of up to about 15.2 m (50 ft) in length. Otherwise, very substantial and expensive rollers would have to be used.

Roll over hoops, as illustrated in Fig 51, could be used on almost any size of vessel. They consist of a fairly heavy channel section shaped in a curve, not necessarily a segment of a circle, or they could even be a series of flats. For rigidity, the completed hoop is secured to the hull and the building jig, and one or preferably two cranes, or lifting chain tackles if a small craft, are secured to the base of each hoop on one side and lifts. When lifted to beyond top dead centre, the whole unit completes the journey to upright position by its own weight. Fig 52 illustrates the operation.

FIG 52 *Turning over a 22.8 m (75 ft) hull.*

8 • FABRICATION AND SETTING UP

The design will, to a very large extent, determine the fabrication and setting up of the vessel. Certain aspects need to be considered at this stage: What items are intercostal and which continuous? Are bulkheads watertight? Are there integral tanks? Is the design based on longitudinal or transverse framing or a combination of both? Is the vessel to be built by unit construction? What lifting gear is available? Will it be built upside down? We must even consider at this stage how the vessel will be launched.

The shipyard manager must, before the job is started, plan each sequence of operations, starting at launching, and provide a logical regression of events. This may not be so necessary with smaller boats, say under 12.2 m (40 ft), but when the overall length is longer than 18.2 m (60 ft) and launching weight over 30 tons (30.5 tonnes), a general plan is essential. The actual details can be decided as the job progresses. But it would be very unfortunate, for example, to build the vessel upside down and then find it cannot be turned over because of lack of gear or space. When setting up it is not enough to be planning just the next step: two or three steps ahead must be considered. Many pitfalls can be avoided with such forward thinking.

The laying off, and making of templates, has been described in Chapter 6. Using the bulkhead templates, mark off the outline with a scriber on to the appropriate plates, and then cut out and weld. As the welding proceeds, check for distortion and correct it. If the design calls for stiffeners running in one direction only, say vertical, it may be necessary to weld on temporary stiffeners horizontally to counteract the transverse distortion that would otherwise occur. In welding large flat areas such as full bulkheads, it is very easy to build in distortion unless precautions are taken. The largest plates possible should be used and sequences adopted, as described in Chapter 4, to minimise distortion. Any large holes or openings for doorways should be cut out after all the welding has been completed. The same procedure should be used for the engine beds if, as is usual, they form part of the main structure.

Before erection of any of the bulkheads, datum lines must be transferred from the templates on to the bulkheads with lightly scribed lines. These will normally consist of the centreline, datum waterline, and a level line near the sheer line.

Assuming the boat is to be built upside down, consideration must be given as to whether the deck should be constructed, and used as a jig for setting up the bulkheads and frames, or whether a separate jig should be used. It is probably more straightforward, though a little more expensive on materials, to build on a separate jig. Transverses will have been secured to the jig in way of all frame and bulkhead stations, a centreline will be prominently marked on all transverses, and the jig will be set up level longitudinally and transversely. A spirit level alone is not sufficiently accurate over long distances. A water level, or preferably a surveyor's level, should be used instead. If we are to use the jig (and it is sensible to do so) as our datum for setting up the framing, it is essential that this be level all ways. Before setting up can commence, a common distance must be decided upon from the level line on the framing to a common level on the jig. This should be determined by allowing a minimum gap of about 45 cm (18 in) between the lowest part of the sheer and the jig, so that when the plating is in position there is sufficient room left for someone to crawl through.

The main bulkheads and transom may now be erected on the appropriate stations, making sure that the centreline and level line are in accord with the jig. A plumb bob will be used to position the centreline, and a water level for the level lines. Temporary steel angles, through bolted, should connect the bulkheads to the jig and be securely stayed with struts. If, as is often the case, the minor frames are intercostal to the keel and engine beds, the keel and engine beds should now be erected and welded in position. We now have a backbone, and terminal points to which we can attach the frames (see Fig 53). Level lines should be scribed to all frames prior to erection. There will be many times later when it is necessary to obtain a positioning datum within the hull, and this is the most accurate way to obtain it. When all the bulkheads, transom, engine beds, and frames are in position, stringers, chines, and gunwales should be prepared. When the stringers are slotted into the frames, and the laying off is to a very high standard, the stringer slots could be cut into the frames prior to erection. Should there be doubt as to precise accuracy, the stringer slots should be faired in after frame erection and cut out. It may take a little longer to cut in the slots, but it saves time should the slots need repositioning and the redundant holes plugged. Now is the time, while there is still accessibility, to fit the interior bracketry that is normally called for on the design. Wherever possible, welding in way of integral tanks should be carried out before the restrictions of plating. The framework must now be faired prior to plating, and this is done with a dreadnought file, or grinder. It must be carefully carried out with constant checking with fairing batten, athwartships and longitudinally. It is very easy to fair the frames and find there is a hollow in the stringers at that point, or vice versa. It is this operation that very largely determines the shape of the hull. Any unfairness in the structure will be transferred to the plating and will be very difficult to eradicate.

Waterways should be cut into the structure on the bottom; this will enable the bilge water to drain to the strum boxes.

The shell expansion drawing will indicate where the plating butts pass

FIG 53 *Early erection of framing.*

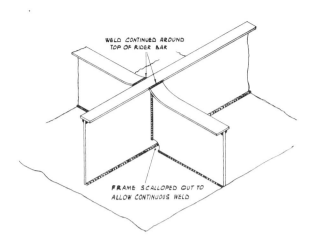

WELD CONTINUED AROUND
TOP OF RIDER BAR

FRAME SCALLOPED OUT TO
ALLOW CONTINUOUS WELD

FIG 54 *Welding continuity.*

FIG 55 *Welding must progress evenly from side to side.*

through the stringers and frames. Notches should be cut out to enable the welding to be continuous (see Fig 54).

During the whole period of frame erection a constant check should be kept on the centreline of the keel. This must be maintained in a straight line, so that a steering bias does not get built in. Welding must progress evenly from side to side (see Fig 55), aiming constantly at equalisation or cancellation of welding stresses. This also applies to engine beds, which should be kept as straight as possible. If shaft tunnels are called for, these also should be fitted and welded in position.

If the vessel is to be built right side up, the procedure is generally similar, except that the keel and stem are laid down first and the bulkheads erected on them. Two verticals well braced and slightly further apart than the length of the boat, and slightly higher than the sheer, with a taut wire stretched between

them, provides a datum from which a plumb bob can be suspended to centre the keel and stem, and align the centreline of the bulkheads.

The keel will be set up either on keel blocks, a little taller than the launching trolley to enable it to be positioned after plating is completed, or on the launching trolley itself. The practice of the yard and availability of lifting gear will more or less predetermine your choice. The building base should preferably be set up level longitudinally to the waterlines, as this will allow plain spirit levels to be used during construction, and it can also be used to obtain a vertical datum from a waterline. If this is not possible, a declination piece will have to be added to the base of the spirit level, at the same incline as the waterlines. This can be a great nuisance and should be avoided if possible. With the keel and stem well secured in position with temporary struts, a main bulkhead as near midships as possible should be erected. This will be our master bulkhead, and great care should be exercised to ensure that it is upright and set at 90° to the centreline of the keel. The sheer and chine, or bilge, should be horned in to the centreline of the stem – eg the opposite point on the bulkhead should measure the same amount of the stem. When this master bulkhead is correctly and securely positioned, the other bulkheads, moving forward and aft, can be positioned in relation to it. Engine beds, frames and stringers will follow as previously described.

9 ◆ HULL PLATING

The designer and builder will already have agreed the general overall size of the hull plates, and the shell expansion drawing indicating the position of all the butts will have been issued. Commensurate with the lifting gear available and the curvature of the hull, the largest available sheets should be used. This will obviously reduce the amount of welding, thus saving time, and will usually result in a fairer hull. However, it is sometimes necessary to use small sizes of sheet because of lack of availability. When this is the case, as much welding should be done off the job as is practicable. This will enable backing bars to be used, with a single pass. Usually this results in a neater weld that requires less cleaning, and a stronger weld with less faults.

Where a high standard of lofting is available, laying off or marking the perimeter of the plates is not a problem, as this can be done direct from the loft floor or scrieve board. Where there is doubt, it will be necessary either to lift the plates in position, or make templates, to suit the marks on the framing that have been transferred from the shell expansion drawing. The cheapest quality of

FIG 56 Philante VIII, *an aluminium alloy motor yacht built for Tommy Sopwith by Souter to a Shead design, on trials in the Solent* (Photo: Souter Shipyard).

hardboard is suitable for this, and gives a fair indication of how the aluminium sheet will lie in position and whether much shaping will be required.

Whether to commence plating from the sheer or keel is largely a matter of personal preference. If the vessel is built upside down it may be easier to start from the keel down, but if the boat is built right way up it may be simpler to work from the sheer down. This will provide easier access to the inside of the hull for a longer period. One advantage of building upside down is that when plating, especially the bottom on a chine boat, the plates will rest in position without the necessity for external supports. All that is needed are a few cramps around the perimeter. For plates of up to about 8 mm (just over $\frac{1}{4}$ in) where the curvature is small and regular, cramps are normally all that is necessary to pull the plate to the framing. It is better to pull the plates down under a little pressure as this will ensure they are touching down on the centre, and it gives a fairer line to the finished hull. For plates thicker than this, and where there are complex curves, it will be necessary to shape the plates. The really thick plates, in excess of 12 mm (about $\frac{1}{2}$ in), are normally only required in way of propeller brackets, and these require rolling only because they are at the far aft end. Where double curvature occurs, it may be necessary to use the wheeling machine to provide 'belly' in the centre of the plate, and if the periphery needs a little shrinking this can quite simply be done on the Eckold shaper. Putting shape into an aluminium plate, provided the right gear and a little knowhow is available, should not be a great problem. It is not necessary or desirable to shape the contour of the hull completely, as the final pulling down to shape should be left to the cramps.

FIG 57 *America's Cup contender* Lionheart *under construction at Joyce Marine in 1979. All hull plates are tacked in position before final welding proceeds* (Photo: Eckold Ltd).

Where there is plating of different thicknesses, it is easier to put the thicker plates in position first, especially if, as is usual, the extra thickness has to be removed from the framing to allow a flush exterior. At the initial stage, all the plates should be tacked into position first to minimise distortion, and also you may need to remove one if, for instance, it is not laying fair. Both sides of the hull should be worked simultaneously or alternately for equalisation of welding stresses.

For plate butts that have to be welded on the hull, one of three methods can be used:

1 A permanent backing bar can either be built into the hull, or a part of structure could be used as such. The backer would have to be welded to the skin, but there is no simple way of checking the degree of penetration.

2 A MIG root pass is laid on the inside of the skin, back chipped, and the final pass or passes laid on the outside.

3 A TIG root pass is laid from the outside of the skin, back chipped, and the final pass or passes are laid on the outside. If TIG is available, it would probably result in a neater job and require less cleaning up.

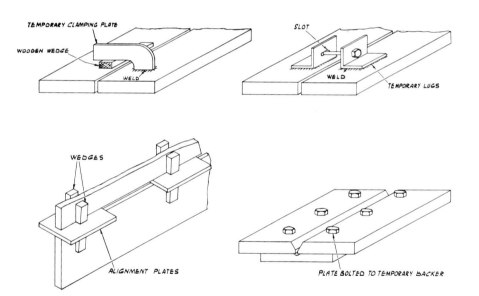

FIG 58 *Simple plate welding jigs.*

There are many and various small aids, most of them fabricated from scrap, that the operator can make for himself to assist in the precise placing and positioning of the plates. Some of these are shown in Fig 58. These usually incorporate some kind of wedge that will force the butts together longitudinally and vertically while they are being tacked. They can then be dispensed with when full welding takes place. If the gap between the butts permits, small bolts with washer plates and nuts could be inserted and screwed up tight. Provided it does not create distortion, there is no objection to passing a temporary bolt through the centre of the plate to pull down locally. The hole can quite easily be filled with TIG afterwards.

Where a large number of boats are to be built to a standard design and the hull

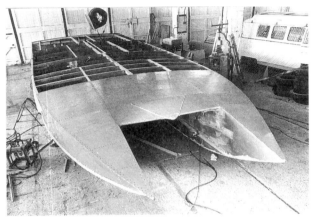

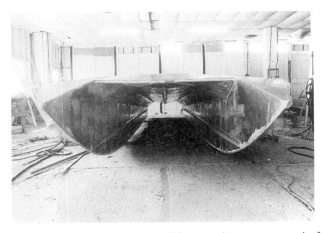

FIG 59 Above: Romans Sabre, *a 9.7 m (32 ft) offshore racing catamaran in frame. All the frames are one piece to maintain rigidity. Note the small step in the bottom to reduce skin friction. Design by James Beard.* Centre: *1.5 mm ($\frac{1}{16}$ in) riveted deck and topsides with towing plate in position. Twin Sabre diesel engines provide the power.* Below: Romans Sabre's *hull is completed. A view through the tunnel showing the vertical insides to the twin hulls and integral bridge deck. The spray rail angle bar is welded to the inside of the hulls.*

shape is complex, aluminium is the ideal material for pre-forming. For large-scale production, it pays to indulge in cost-cutting methods, even though it involves a considerable investment in tools and equipment. Bending or shaping plates, or any other part of the structure, for quantity production can be accomplished in one of three or a combination of the three methods, depending on the complexity of the shape, the size of the section, and the number to be produced. The three methods are: pressbrake, hydraulic rubber press, and stretch forming.

Pressbrake

No great expenditure is required if the pressbrake is available. A simple wooden punch and die is used as a top and bottom tool. The aluminium sheet is sandwiched between them and pressure applied. The size of plate and amount of curvature would be somewhat restricted, and the tool would have a limited life. Its virtue is simplicity and low cost, but it is not very accurate.

Hydraulic rubber press

Rubber press work requires considerably more pressure than is normally provided with a pressbrake. It has a larger rubber bed which is often almost square. Only a punch or top tool is required. The punch presses the aluminium into the rubber, which squeezes it around the punch until it takes the form of the punch. It is sometimes necessary to overbend to allow for springback.

Stretch forming

A stretch forming machine is, depending on the size of plate to be worked, very large, powerful and expensive. The stretch forming operation consists of gripping the sheet tautly at opposite edges, and forcing a form block of the required shape into it. This is usually done in two stages. The sheet is first stressed to just below the yield point, then given an additional stretch to obtain a permanent set. There is very little springback, and the formed parts show little or no distortion. Unlike normal bending, which compresses the metal at the inside of the curve and stretches that on the outside, the stretch former forms entirely by tension, elongating the metal beyond the elastic limit. This also raises the yield point, so that a stress greater than that originally used to form the shape is required to deform it.

FIG 60 *Keel and chine section.*

Only a large number of formed parts justifies the initial expenditure, but stretch formers are used in other industries, particularly the aircraft industry,

AS CHINE SECTION   AS KEEL SECTION   AS GUNWALE SECTION

and sometimes time on a machine can be hired. Stretch forming to an appropriate shape can so stiffen a hull that very little internal structure is required. It is possible to form the whole side of a boat in one operation.

For smaller vessels an extruded section at keel, chine or gunwale can be used (see Fig 60). This has the advantage of trapping and forming a strong edge to the plating, which in turn is welded to it. Where a multi-conic design is used, the plating should wrap around the structure without any problem.

While the plating is progressing, it is sometimes advantageous to build in the integral tanks and shaft tunnels, because the welder will have greater access to some joints that are otherwise very difficult to get at. If the vessel is built upside down, and spray rails are called for, these should be fully welded in position before turning the boat over.

10 ◆ DECKING

Decks perform many functions, and the scantlings and design must be carefully considered so that areas of high local stress are adequately provided for. The deck forms the upper flange of the main hull girder. It must be watertight to maintain the integrity of the watertight hull, and have permanent or temporary means of closing all openings in the exposed portions. Openings are required for personal access, and also to allow the removal of machinery when necessary. In addition, there are openings with suitable protection to provide light and air.

Weather decks are normally cambered with a parabolic curve to give added strength and so shed water quickly. They may be framed transversely or longitudinally – or even, as often occurs, a combination of both. Where normally the deck transverses support the longitudinals, then longitudinals, frames and deck beams need only be welded intermittently to each other and to the underside of the deck. Where very high local stresses may occur – such as gun mountings or mast steps – a deep transverse immediately under the stress location can be further strengthened with a pillar to a main framing member on the bottom of the hull (consideration must of course be given to the effect this would have on the accommodation below).

Hatch openings should be surrounded by deep coamings with radiused or elliptical corners, in order to reduce stress concentrations. The greatest longitudinal bending stresses occur over the midship region. To accommodate this, the greatest deck plate thickness is maintained over 40 per cent of the length amidships, and tapers to a minimum thickness at the bow and stern.

Decks can be covered with wood sheathing or a plastic deck covering such as

FIG 61 Left: *Typical bulwark capping.*
FIG 62 Right: *Hawse hole ring.*

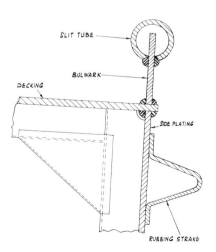

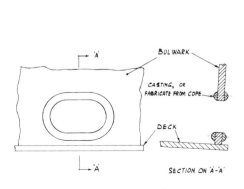

Trakmark or Treadmaster. This not only improves the appearance, but provides a non-slip surface and protection from heat – especially in the accommodation areas where heat can be quite considerable. Direct contact of the wood deck to aluminium should be used with discretion, because of the possibility of a slight corrosive effect. This sometimes occurs with oak and some of the tropical hardwoods. This can be minimised by bedding the wood on to either a bituminous compound, a butyl rubber compound, or a resin system, which would also act as an adhesive. If it is necessary to secure the wood with through fastenings, these should be counterbored and the dowels glued. Trakmark and Treadmaster are supplied with their own resin adhesives, which should be applied after the aluminium has been cleaned and degreased.

Bulwarks are often fitted forward. This not only improves appearance, but gives some personal protection when on the foredeck. These are either an extension of the side plating, or are welded on after the decking margin plate is fitted.

If the bulwarks are tall, they may need stiffening brackets, but usually they are stiff enough by themselves. Should they sustain heavy blows they would probably cause less damage to the deck if brackets are not fitted. The top edge of the bulwark can be protected and stiffened by fitting half round cope, or preferably a split pipe as shown in Fig 61.

Scuppers should be cut at the bottom for drainage, and hawse holes for mooring lines. If these are large, they should have some strengthening round the edge – either a simple sand casting or fabrication (see Fig 62).

11 ◆ SUPERSTRUCTURES

Because of the prominent position of deck structures, they must be aesthetically pleasing as well as functional. Careful design can produce a very light and strong structure. Weight saving, particularly above deck level, is a very desirable feature; overall displacement is reduced with its many benefits, and stability is increased. Aluminium is a very popular material for constructing deckhouses, and there are probably more such deck-houses fitted to vessels of every description than those made of any other single material. It is very common practice to fit aluminium superstructures to steel hulls, and a typical method of securing to the hull is shown in Fig 63. A properly designed shell of, say, 2–3 mm (about $\frac{1}{8}$ in), though of adequate strength, can sometimes cause production problems. There are occasions when, because of complex shapes, riveting is not acceptable for appearance's sake or practical reasons. Several rows of rivets on an otherwise unblemished spherical surface are not always pleasing to the eye, especially when each rivet causes a slight flattening under the head. In these circumstances, welding is the only answer (see Fig 66).

An experienced welder, using the correct procedures, should have little trouble in producing an acceptable finish. A complex shape will, to an extent, assist in resisting distortion. The shell, including the stiffening, should be tack welded before full welding is commenced. The window openings should not be cut out until all welding has been completed. Depending on operator efficiency, TIG would probably be more suitable. With all the sheets fair and tack welded in position, final welding can begin. Until you have worked out a successful technique, proceed with extra caution. The following suggestions may help:

1 Do not overweld, and weld only a few centimetres at a time to start with. Do not make an adjacent weld until the first has cooled.

FIG 63 Left: *Typical method of securing alloy superstructure to steel deck.*

FIG 64 Right: *Typical method of securing superstructure on an all-alloy boat.*

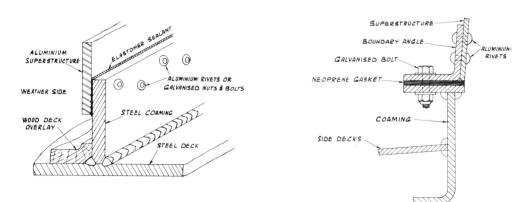

FIG 65 *A 2.6 mm ($\frac{1}{8}$ in) thick swaged aluminium alloy superstructure skin on a 35 m (114 ft) motor yacht. Stiffening sections are formed by a pressbrake* (Photo: Shead Design).

2 Work alternately port and starboard to equalise contraction stresses. If during the initial tacking the butts were too tight with insufficient gap, and subsequently distortion is now occurring, it may be necessary to cut all the tacks in that butt and start again with spacers in the seam. It should be realised that this type of condition always deteriorates as welding proceeds.

3 Riveting is the obvious choice where there are large flat areas. Without shape to give rigidity, welding thin gauges would inevitably cause distortion problems. It is possible, though, to combine welding and riveting quite successfully.

4 Riveted butt joints normally require four rows of rivets (two rows staggered each side). Where this is objected to on the grounds of appearance, the butt could be welded using part of the main structure as a permanent backer.

5 The centre and perimeter of the panel could then be riveted. The ideal extrusion for interior structure for riveting is a 'zed' section. This provides a riveting flange and an interior stiffening flange, to which linings can be attached, and the intervening space can be filled with insulation. It is not easy to shape 'zeds' and maintain a fair line, so they are restricted to straight lines. If the curves are produced conically, there is of course no problem.

6 Which type of rivet to use is to some extent a matter of preference, and this is discussed more fully in Chapter 5 under riveting.

7 Various fittings such as radio aerials, loud hailers, searchlights, radar scanners, etc are frequently installed on the wheel-house roof, often as an afterthought.

8 It is essential, if the structure is of a light gauge, that local stiffening, commensurate with the load it has to carry, should be built in as the erection proceeds.

9 To secure the deck-house in position, it is normal to rivet a ground angle to the base of the structure and bolt this to the deck, or preferably to the coaming around the periphery, with a suitable neoprene type gasket between the mating surfaces to ensure watertightness (see Fig 64).

10 If the deck-house is large, or has a complex shape, it would probably be

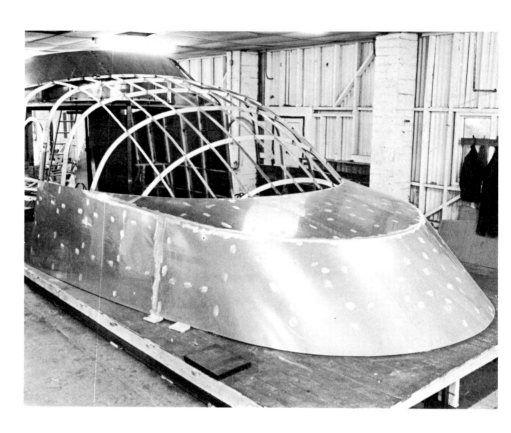

FIG 66 *Welded superstructure of complex shape.*

advantageous to build it off the boat. This would enable the construction to proceed at the same time as the hull, and it would save a great deal of climbing time. A simple mock up of the deck, or base upon which it will eventually be seated, is required – and this can also serve as a base for a jig. Depending to a large extent on the shape or complexity of the deck-house, the jig can be of wood, steel or, if a simple shape, the interior structure of the deck-house can be erected and the skin secured directly to it. Where there is a lot of shape, a wooden jig is often more suitable. The panels would be shaped around this, then the interior structure shaped to suit the panels (see Fig 66).

When the superstructure is built off the boat, consideration must be given to lifting it to its final position. It is not always possible or advisable to lift a large structure in one piece. Transport joints should be built into the structure as construction proceeds. These should, wherever possible, be at strong points such as master frames or bulkheads. They will be bolted at watertight pitch with bedding compound on faying surfaces. Lifting lugs can be riveted or bolted, preferably in way of bulkheads.

Care must be taken when lifting that a crushing or squeezing load is not forced upon the structure. This can be avoided by using lifting beams that will ensure a direct vertical pull on the lifting points (see Fig 67).

When the superstructure is built directly above the engine space, it is necessary to incorporate hatches in the flooring and the roof of the structure, large enough to allow access for the engines, both for installation and subsequent removal.

FIG 67 *A lifting beam ensures a direct vertical pull.*

12 ✦ ANCILLARY STRUCTURES

Apart from aluminium's use in the hull and superstructure, there are many economic and functional advantages to be gained from its other marine applications.

The weight saving can be considerable, and there is the advantage of complete compatibility with the aluminium hull. Perhaps more than any other metal, aluminium lends itself to fabrication – provided, that is, the proper equipment is available. Much of the material used can be utilised from what would otherwise be scrap. Provided the demand exists, and production and distribution costs are reasonable, an enterprising company could well add considerably to their gross income (with little additional capital investment) through the wider application of aluminium. We are, however, concerned here only with those items that have a direct application to boatbuilding, some of which are now detailed.

Masts and spars

Apart from the normal round tube extrusions, there are many other special mast extrusions available – some with internal or external integral sail tracks. With a little judicious vee-shaped cutting and welding, these can be tapered to reduce weight and windage. They can also be formed on a pressbrake or roll formed. Extruded mast tracks can be added externally. Some typical shapes are shown in Fig 68. Aluminium lugs and cleats may be cast or cut from sheet or extruded sections for attaching standing and running rigging. It is normal to anodise the

FIG 68 *Typical mast extrusions.*

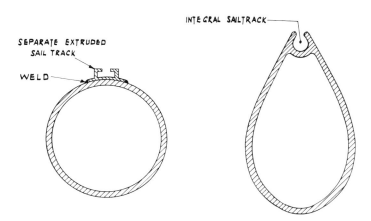

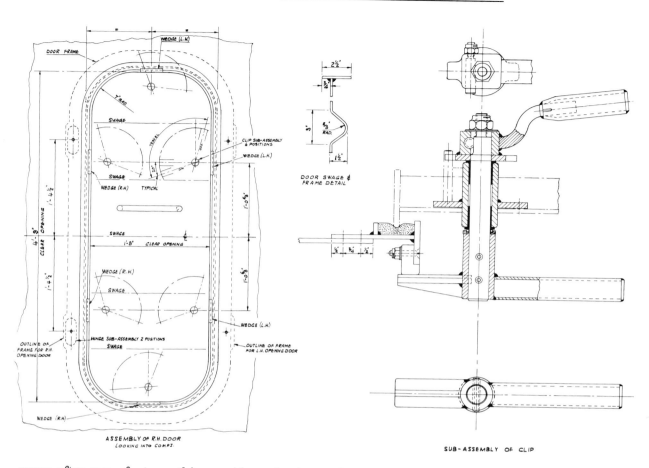

ASSEMBLY OF R.H. DOOR
LOOKING INTO COMPT.

DOOR SWAGE &
FRAME DETAIL

SUB-ASSEMBLY OF CLIP

spars after manufacture; this provides a lasting and pleasing finish, with no other treatment being required.

FIG 69 *Arrangement of watertight door.*

Tanks

Fuel and water tanks are frequently made of aluminium, irrespective of the hull material. The interiors of fuel tanks, both diesel and petrol, are often left unpainted, but freshwater tanks are sometimes treated internally with a special composition to reduce the possibility of the slightly tainted taste that can occur over time. Sewage and sanitary tanks, particularly if they are integral, should be coated internally with a bitumastic solution such as Proderite. If the metal is left bare, a gradual corrosive effect may result.

Ladders

Special hollow extrusions are produced for ladders or they can be fabricated from plate and tube. Unless large-scale output is envisaged, it would probably be uneconomic to set up a production process for this. Purchasing from specialist manufacturers who produce in very large quantities, normally at very economic prices, would probably prove cheaper.

Watertight doors

These are normally quite straightforward and could very easily be produced by boatbuilders. Swages are often formed in the door panel to provide the same strength with lighter gauge material. Handles can either be fabricated or be simple sand castings. A typical section is shown in Fig 69.

Window frames

Many extruded sections are produced for the various types of windows: fixed, half drop, sliding and hinged. Radius corners are formed on special-purpose tooling and mitred corners are welded. Weather seals can also be obtained for fitting into the fixed or sliding-type frames. These may be silicone-treated wool-pile seals, polyethylene guides or vinyl weatherstripping (see Fig 70).

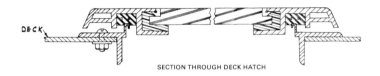

SECTION THROUGH DECK HATCH

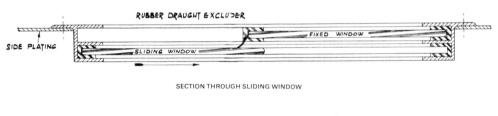

SECTION THROUGH SLIDING WINDOW

SECTION THROUGH FIXED WINDOW

FIG 70 *Weather seals.*

Wherever possible, safety glass should be installed in the frames, particularly if they are large, and/or forward facing. It is sometimes necessary to accept plastic glazing for curved frames. This is not really desirable as the plastic is normally a good deal softer than glass and more susceptible to scratches, which in time tend to decrease visibility. If the vessel is to be used in the Mediterranean or eastern waters where sunlight is particularly bright, it is recommended that you use a tinted glass such as ICI 911. This, while not impeding visibility, reduces glare and heat penetration. All frames should be anodised to retain their bright appearance.

Windscreens or windshields, arranged as a protection on the external flying bridge, may have brackets that are simply fabricated from aluminium sheet (similar to that shown in Fig 71). Where the eye level is above the top of the screen, these may be in plastic such as acrylic or perspex. They would be considerably cheaper than glass and, when damaged, more easily replaced. Opening

portlights and deadlight frames are usually castings and are available in many shapes, sizes and types. Unless the required item is not obtainable from suppliers, it is probably cheaper to buy them.

FIG 71 *Aluminium sheet brackets for windscreens.*

Deck fittings

A very wide variety of deck fittings are obtainable from marine manufacturers. For items such as fairleads, cleats and bollards, where a high-quality yacht finish is required, these are probably best purchased as castings. However, they can be very expensive if supplied with a highly polished finish. If you want cheaper fittings, they can sometimes be obtained from the foundry in an 'as cast' condition. Such fittings are fairly smooth, but lack the brilliance of a polished surface. They would normally be acceptable on commercial or service craft. Where an even cheaper fitting is required, these can be fabricated quite cheaply from offcuts of tube and plate (as in Fig 72).

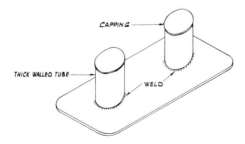

Deck fillers with screwed caps are readily available as castings to suit from 2.5 cm (1 in) to 5 cm (2 in) pipe. For sizes outside this range, tube and plate welded would be satisfactory, but the screwed filler cap would have to be fairly thick to allow for the thread and deck key.

FIG 72 *Fabricated bollards.*

Handrails are simply made from tube, with the fittings, sockets and brackets being either castings or fabrications.

Side deck stanchions are made from tube with the top blanked off, and where wire rope passes through the stanchion, a small insert tube should be welded in to eliminate chafing of the wire. Deck stanchion sockets, where a number are required, should be obtained as castings. If less than about ten are required, tube welded on to plate would suffice. A drain hole should be drilled close to the base and a drop nose pin with keep chain secures the stanchion in the socket.

Hawse pipes that pass through the deck as leads for the anchor chain and anchor are fabricated from large tube, to suit the individual requirement. The end of the tube that secures to the stem or side plate should have a heavy reinforcement to withstand the chain wear. A typical example is illustrated in Fig 73.

Ventilators of the cowl type are normally pressed into shape or spun, but are beyond the scope of the average boatbuilder. Mushroom ventilators can be produced by most boatbuilders, but unless they are fairly large – more than 15 cm (6 in) in diameter – they are not economical to produce in small numbers.

FIG 73 *Prefabricated hawse pipe.*

Aluminium ducting for air conditioning is almost the standard, irrespective of hull material. Its light weight, easy formability, and resistance to the effect of the moisture that is inevitably present in the system, make it the ideal material.

Boxes containing electrical control switch gear, fuses, distributors, rectifiers, transformers, circuit breakers, etc, and instrument panels for the various meters and switches, are very easily produced with the aid of a folder. Because aluminium is non-magnetic, it can be used in close proximity to the magnetic compass without producing a deviation effect.

Aluminium fuel piping, freshwater piping and bilge pipes are frequently installed. Joints are easily made with cone nuts or flanged joints. Small diameter pipes up to about 1.2 cm ($\frac{1}{2}$ in) diameter are easily bent around a hand former without filling. Larger diameters require filling with Sarabend, or a similar product, to prevent kinking.

Deck boxes for the stowage of ropes, fend-offs, etc can very easily be formed in aluminium, and riveted or welded – often from material that would otherwise be scrap.

13 ◆ Painting

Painting has two general functions to perform: protection and cosmetic appearance. Of the two, protection is the more important as it may well affect the life and service of the vessel.

Protective coatings

This can also be broken down under two headings: protection against electrolytic action by the proximity of dissimilar metals, and protection of the ship's underwater plating by the fouling of natural marine growth.

ELECTROLYTIC ACTION

As explained in Chapter 14 on corrosion, two dissimilar metals in an electrolyte set up an electric cell with the more active or anodic metal tending to disintegrate. One way of stopping this from causing real damage is to fit sacrificial anodes. This, though, is only really necessary where an electrolyte – eg seawater – is present, normally on the outside of the hull. However, there are other places – inside the hull and topsides for example – that will also need protection, for although the process is greatest in seawater itself, a salt atmosphere can also have an effect. A suitable paint scheme will very effectively isolate the two surfaces and, while intact, will eliminate or minimise any trouble.

It is very good practice to ensure that all faying (mating) surfaces have an insulating layer between them. This will isolate the surfaces and prevent moisture becoming trapped. The insulating material obviously must be inert and suitable for the function it has to perform.

Where an aluminium skin fitting is through bolted to the skin or bulkhead, a thin layer of PRC jointing compound (already described in Chapter 5 on fastenings) or similar should be sandwiched between the two surfaces and around the bolt head and shank. Where it is necessary to pass copper piping or a similar cathodic material through an aluminium bulkhead (as is sometimes called for), as for instance in some air conditioning installations carrying refrigerants, the piping should pass through the bulkhead as high up as possible away from the bilge, and a rubber or neoprene gasket should isolate the copper from the aluminium.

ANTI-FOULING

The sea's surface waters contain an immense amount of floating microscopic animal and plant life, known generally as plankton. Among these plankton are innumerable young (lava) forms of creatures such as barnacles, mussels, etc, which, when they have reached maturity, are found attached to objects below the surface. The plankton also contains millions of spores of various seaweeds.

FIG 74   *A 30 m (98 ft) Solent class 35 knot catamaran in service with Red Funnel Ferries. The craft features round bilge sea-kindly hull forms to maximise passenger comfort at high speed in rough seas* (Photo: FBM Marine Ltd).

All boats in the sea are therefore immersed in this collection of living organisms, a great many of which will settle, if given the chance, on the vessels' hulls and grow into a fouling growth. Although these various forms of growth cannot directly harm the aluminium hull, if left unchecked they can result in a serious loss of speed. Also, by masking the sacrificial anodes and destroying the paint scheme, they could, where dissimilar metals are present, lead to corrosion of the hull. To prevent this fouling of the boat's bottom, it is strongly recommended that it be coated with an anti-fouling compound. The principle underlying the use of anti-fouling products is that as the toxic substances that they contain slowly and constantly dissolve, the ship's surface is permanently surrounded by a thin layer of toxic solution. Therefore if the anti-fouling compound is working properly – ie if the toxic layer is being maintained – the marine growth will be prevented from getting a foothold. The fouling attack always comes from organisms in a microscopic state, so if the film of water in immediate contact with the ship's surface can be kept in a condition toxic to this primitive life, the organisms are destroyed.

The anti-fouling film is, therefore, a storehouse for poisonous materials that are constantly being dissolved by the sea. The poisons most commonly used today are derived from copper, mercury and tin. In addition, some specialised anti-foulings may contain other forms of organic poisons. No paint or composition containing mercury or copper should ever be used on aluminium, even over protective coatings. Mercury is especially dangerous, as it inhibits the formation of a protective coating of oxide; without this, the alloy can rapidly erode. Many paint manufacturers produce a composition that is especially suitable for aluminium. Their advice should be sought and a full paint scheme (including suitable undercoats) applied.

One other form of anti-fouling should be mentioned – tank interiors. Fuel tanks do not need painting. Freshwater tanks, on the other hand, should always be etched and painted because over a period of time fresh water contains certain contaminates that can cause a slime to adhere to the aluminium. This does not harm the aluminium, but it may affect the taste. Sanitary and sewage tanks should also be treated, as they can suffer a corrosive effect; here again, paint manufacturers should be consulted for suitable coatings for each situation.

Decorative painting

The topsides of an aluminium hull need be painted only for appearance's sake. If left bare, a dirty matt-grey finish will result and a white powder will form on the surface. This is a self-protecting salt-like structure that is inherent in the aluminium, but is not harmful.

Aluminium holds paint well, provided that the surface is properly prepared for receiving the undercoats and is applied in thicknesses and under conditions recommended by the paint manufacturer. Most of them suggest that the ideal temperature for painting is between 15°C (60°F) and 26°C (80°F), with relative humidity between 30 per cent and 40 per cent. Regardless of the kind of paint, under high humidity conditions the temperature of the hull should be higher than that of the surrounding air in order to prevent condensation. No painting should be done outside after sundown if there's any possibility of a dew, and never, of course, in a damp atmosphere.

Here is a typical painting specification with materials supplied by International Yacht Paints:

SELF-ETCH PRIMER
Both light alloy and galvanised zinc may have greasy and highly polished surfaces that must be pre-treated before painting. They must first be degreased and then coated with self-etch primer which, in one operation, etches the surface and provides the protective coat. Self-etching primer and its accelerator are supplied separately. Two parts self-etching primer to one part accelerator should be mixed immediately before application and used within eight hours.

The mixture should be applied as a thin wash coat, approximately 13.0 sq m/litre. It is important to note the colour change that takes place after some minutes, indicating that the material has 'taken'. If the colour change does not occur, it is because the underlying metal is not clean enough or because the temperature is too low. In this eventuality you will have to remove the primer with stripper, so do make a point of studying the instructions on the pack carefully before applying the self-etch primer.

Drying time 4 hours.
Apply light alloy primer or metallic primocon 4–24 hours later.
Covering capacity 13.0 sq m/litre.

LIGHT ALLOY PRIMER
Light alloy primer is a corrosion inhibitor and is used over self-etch primer, except below the waterline externally.

Drying time 4 to 6 hours.
Interval between coats 1 to 10 days.
Covering capacity 10 sq m/litre.

METALLIC PRIMOCON

Metallic primocon is used on all underwater surfaces and is compatible with the surface of anti-fouling. The anti-fouling must be applied direct to the primocon.

Drying time 4 hours.
Interval between coats 1 day to 3 weeks.
Covering capacity 12 sq m/litre.

CRUISER COPOLYMER ANTI-FOULING

Especially produced for use on light alloy craft. Should be immersed within 6 weeks of first application.

Drying time 1 hour.
Interval between coats 6 to 24 hours.
Covering capacity 9.8 sq m/litre.
Special thinners No. 3.

WATER TANK BLACK

Ensure that all surfaces are perfectly clean and dry before application. Adequate ventilation must be maintained while painting and throughout the drying period. Before the tank is used, thoroughly flush with fresh water.

Drying time about 6 hours.
Covering capacity 10 sq m/litre.

Painting procedure

EXTERIOR HULL BOTTOM

1 Clean all welds and weld penetration marks. Burnish the total area with graded emery cloth.
2 Degrease with acetone or Maritec.
3 Apply one coat of self-etch primer.
4 After 16 to 24 hours, apply one coat of metallic primocon.
5 At about 24-hour intervals, apply a further four coats of metallic primocon.
6 After 5 days, apply the first coat of anti-fouling.
7 After between 6 to 24 hours, apply the second coat of anti-fouling.

Note (most important):
The following need masking and must *not* be painted:
● Sacrificial anodes
● Propellers
● Propeller shafts

EXTERIOR HULL TOPSIDES AND SUPERSTRUCTURES

1 Clean all welds and weld penetration marks, but do not totally remove the weld beads. Burnish the total area with graded emery cloth.
2 Degrease with acetone or Maritec.
3 Apply one coat of self-etch primer.
4 After 16 to 24 hours, apply one coat of light alloy primer.
5 Face up irregularities with a trowel cement.
6 After 16 to 24 hours, apply a second coat of light alloy primer.
7 After 16 to 24 hours, apply a first coat of undercoat.

8 After 16 to 24 hours, apply a second coat of undercoat.
9 After 16 to 24 hours, apply a first coat of enamel.
10 After 16 to 24 hours, rub down lightly with fine grade emery.
11 Apply a second coat of enamel.

DECKS

For areas that are not covered with a special deck covering such as Tread-master, paint as for the topsides, but the final coat should be either non-slip deck paint or else non-slip grit should be added.

ENGINE ROOM

1 For areas that are covered with insulation, no painting is required (and the insulation should not be painted either).
2 The flooring treadplate should not be painted.
3 Underfloor areas do not need painting.
4 All other exposed areas may be coated with a fire retardant paint.

ACCOMMODATION

1 Plywood linings/bulkheads/partitions/overheads:
(a) All surfaces should be thoroughly rubbed down.
(b) Apply one coat of aluminium wood primer.
(c) Apply two coats of undercoat at intervals of 24 hours.
(d) To overheads, apply two coats of matt finish at intervals of 24 hours.
(e) To sides, apply two coats of enamel at intervals of 24 to 48 hours.
2 Mahogany trim:
(a) All surfaces should be thoroughly rubbed down.
(b) Apply one coat of 20 per cent turpentine and varnish.
(c) At intervals of between 24 to 48 hours, apply four coats of varnish.

Note: Rub down lightly between each coat of paint or varnish to produce a smooth, even finish.

FRESHWATER TANK INTERIOR

1 Degrease.
2 Apply one coat of self-etch primer.
3 After 16 to 24 hours, apply one coat of water tank black.

Whether you apply the paint by brush, roller or spray will largely depend on the practice of the yard and the skills of the operators. Brushing would probably be best for small enclosed areas, and spraying for large areas. Where spraying is used, adjacent areas must of course be masked to prevent overspray.

The type of topcoat to be used – enamel, acrylics, polyurethanes, or epoxide resin compositions – will depend on the type of job and required lifespan. The paint manufacturers should be consulted for your own special requirements.

14 ◆ CORROSION

Corrosion of metals is an electro-chemical reaction in which metals react to become oxides or salts. In other words, the metals have a tendency to return to the ores from which they were originally obtained.

In electrical terms, the process involves the loss of electrons from the metallic atom. This means a tiny electrical current is flowing away from the metal. Different metals have a varying electrical potential and the following table shows their relative positions:

Most active	Magnesium
	Zinc
	Galvanised mild steel
	Aluminium
	Iron
	Steel
	Tin
	Lead
	Brass
	Copper
	Silver
Least active	Gold

When two metals are placed in an electrolyte (eg seawater) and connected electrically, a current will pass from the more active to the least active metal, as a result of their different electrical potentials. If the current is sufficiently strong, the less active metal will cease corroding: in electrical terms, it is *cathodic* to the more active metal which, as the giver of the current, is called the *anode*. In releasing this current, the anode will slowly disintegrate and go into solution. A simple galvanic cell in which a small electric current is passing from the aluminium anode to the copper cathode is illustrated in Fig 75.

The galvanic cell

A single piece of metal may become anodic at one point and cathodic at another. Eventually, a hole will appear at the anode where metal has gone into solution, with current flowing towards the cathodic area. The phenomenon is usually the result of microscopic impurities or discontinuities in the metal. If a pinhole is left in the coating on a metal surface, very rapid corrosion can occur at this point.

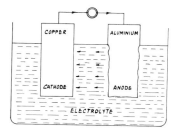

The sacrificial anode

FIG 75 *Galvanic corrosion.*

Anodes vary both in size and composition according to the function they perform. It is the expert's job to advise on the material, shape, size and positioning of the anodes in relation to all other underwater fittings.

The anode chosen will always be electro-negative to the metal it has to protect, and will therefore attract the electric currents present and corrode first. It is not easy to calculate with accuracy the wasting rate of the anode. It should, therefore, be examined at least every six months in the early part of the vessel's life.

Relative areas of cathode and anode are usually as important as, and related to, potential differences. The combination of a large anode, say an aluminium

FIG 76 *A 37 m (121 ft) fast displacement catamaran. The craft has wide sponsons on each hull above the water, reducing to slender hulls at the waterline and widening to circular sections below the waterline* (Photo: FBM Marine Ltd).

hull, and a small cathode, say a manganese bronze propeller, can cause corrosion if the shaft is not also electrically isolated – even if not in direct electrical contact.

It is not always necessary to have dissimilar metals for the creation of these destructive currents. Potential differences can be set up by turbulence and differential aeration, particularly with planing hulls. This must not, of course, be confused with cavitation, which is another subject entirely.

The ideal situation would be to have all underwater fittings of the same metal, and then there would be little likelihood of corrosion. At the moment this is not possible, but there are many things that can be done to ease the situation:

- Seacocks can now be obtained in aluminium and plastic.
- Shaft bearings can be rubber encased in a hard plastic or stainless steel shell, thus insulating the shaft from the hull.
- All underwater fittings and through fastenings should be of compatible material and bedded down on a suitable bedding compound.
- A full and proper paint scheme should be applied, together with a suitable anti-fouling.
- No paint containing mercury or copper should ever be used.
- Several paint manufacturers produce an anti-fouling compound that is especially suitable for aluminium.
- When painting underwater, the sacrificial anodes must not, of course, be painted, as this does inhibit their use.

There are many cases where alloy fittings such as window frames have corroded very badly. Often this is not the result of electrolytic action, but because of the use of an alloy unsuited to withstanding the chemical action of salt spray.

Internal electric currents can also be a source of corrosion. These can be guarded against by the correct installation and insulation of all wiring and auxiliary motors. The installation of the DC current system should be fully insulated with an earth return wire and not earthed through the hull; if this is not done, a fault in the system could cause a current to pass through the hull and thus create corrosion problems.

If precautions are not taken, corrosion can become a major problem, but this need not be so. If it is recognised as a potential hazard at the design stage, and the appropriate action taken by seeking advice from a competent authority, the problem can be reduced to minimal proportions. The points raised in this chapter have, by necessity, been general, and each vessel requires separate analysis.

In considering corrosion, one has to think of its effects over a period of many years. It is then that you realise the importance of taking steps to prevent it.

15 ◆ STERNGEAR

The term 'sterngear' as used here covers the normal external underwater items in power craft that contribute to turning and motion. It includes rudders, tailshafts, shaft brackets and propellers.

The type, design and material used depend to a large extent on the power, speed, size and function of the vessel. The materials should, in so far as is possible, be compatible with the aluminium hull. It is often necessary, though, to make a compromise between compatibility and strength of material.

A copper base material, though not desirable, can be used with discretion, provided that the ratio of the area of the cathodic material (copper) is minimal compared with that of the anodic material (aluminium), and provided that they are physically separated, with sacrificial plates fitted.

FIG 77 *Exterior of a twin water jet assembly protected by a stern platform on a 35 m (114 ft) motor yacht* (Photo: Shead Design).

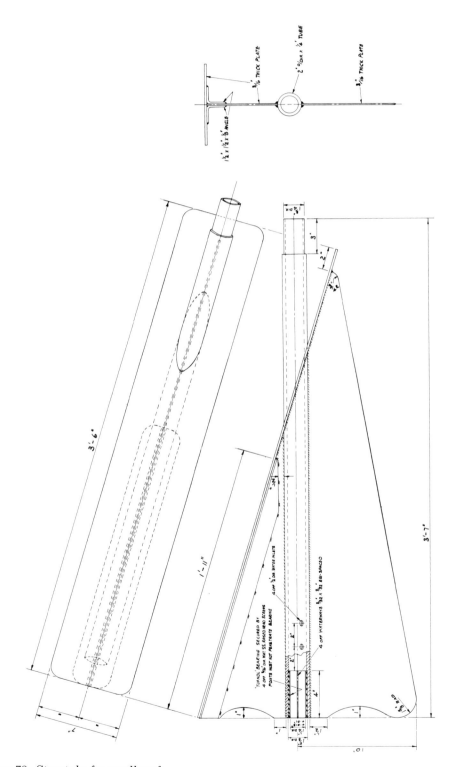

FIG 78 *Sterntube for small craft.*

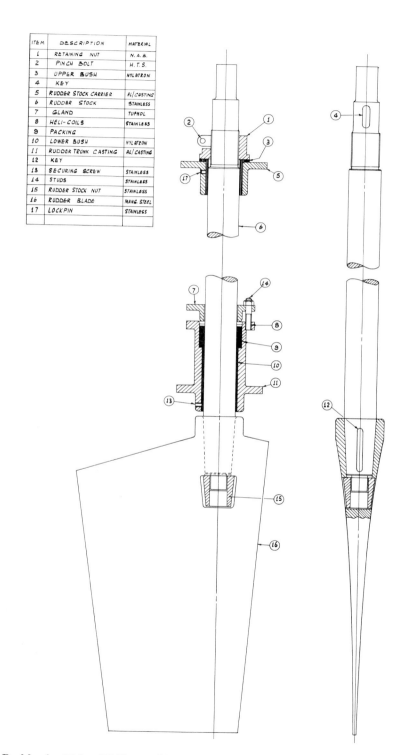

ITEM	DESCRIPTION	MATERIAL
1	RETAINING NUT	N.A.B.
2	PINCH BOLT	H.T.S.
3	UPPER BUSH	NYLATRON
4	KEY	
5	RUDDER STOCK CARRIER	AL/CASTING
6	RUDDER STOCK	STAINLESS
7	GLAND	TUFNOL
8	HELI-COILS	STAINLESS
9	PACKING	
10	LOWER BUSH	NYLATRON
11	RUDDER TRUNK CASTING	AL/CASTING
12	KEY	
13	SECURING SCREW	STAINLESS
14	STUDS	STAINLESS
15	RUDDER STOCK NUT	STAINLESS
16	RUDDER BLADE	MANG. STEEL
17	LOCKPIN	STAINLESS

FIG 79   *Rudder for 22.8 m (75 ft) patrol boat.*

TAILSHAFTS

These are often made of one of the stainless steels, preferably the 18/8 austenitic type. The strength of this material is not very great (about 35 UTS), so if a stronger material is required one of the Aquamet or Monel metals is used. These have a much greater strength factor, and by careful selection can be reasonably compatible.

SHAFT BRACKETS

When required as a casting these will normally be in a cast steel. The specification of the material depends on the strength factors required. For a high speed craft, requiring the minimum cross-sectional area, a manganese steel could be used. The bearing in the bracket would be of the rubber 'cutless' type, bonded to a plastic or stainless steel outer shell, and not the more usual brass type outer shell.

Where a smaller diameter shaft (3.8 cm ($1\frac{1}{2}$ in) or less) is sufficient with moderate horsepower (up to about 50 hp), a simple arrangement with plate and tube could be used, similar to that shown in Fig 78.

Tufnol or lignum-vitae bearings may be used, provided a natural flow of water can be maintained for lubrication. Where the vessel is normally used in sand- or grit-laden waters, a rubber bearing is considered superior and longer lasting.

RUDDERS

For the larger, faster craft, the blades will probably be in cast steel similar to the shaft brackets, with a stainless steel stock. The interior stock and bearing housings are cast aluminium, similar to those in Fig 79. For the smaller, slower craft, a stainless steel stock with either stainless steel or aluminium plate blade is

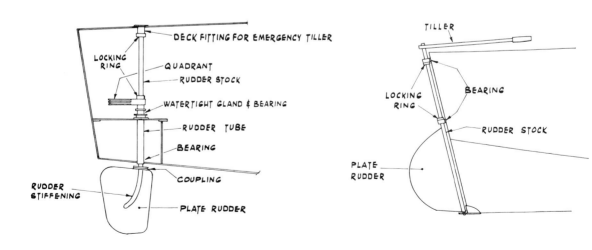

FIG 80   Left: *Sterngear for medium-power small craft.*
FIG 81   Right: *Rudder blade for sailing boat.*

used, as illustrated in Fig 80. There are, of course, a great many variations of blade shape and size. The variable that determines this is the speed of craft, cost, power, whether twin engined and twin rudders, underwater shape of hull, displacement and material. A sailing vessel will have an entirely different blade shape and area, and may well be hung on the transom, as in Fig 81.

PROPELLERS

For small craft with engines up to about 200 hp, a Z-drive transom unit is ideal. This is because the leg, which includes steering and propeller, is of aluminium alloy and therefore normally compatible with an aluminium hull.

Stainless steel in one of its various forms and specifications is also a good propeller material. When bronze propellers must be used, chromium plating will tend to minimise corrosion problems. If the vessel is not normally afloat when not in use, or if used only in fresh water, the problem of dissimilar metals is not so great, and the restrictions thus imposed can – with discretion – be relaxed.

16 ✦ FITTING OUT

The arrangement and assembly of accommodation areas in an aluminium hull differs little from those in any other type of hull structure. Where the interior fit-out and linings are made of wood, wood grounds are usually secured to the aluminium frames. Fastenings would usually be of galvanised mild steel. Under certain climatic conditions, a metal hull will suffer more from condensation than a wooden hull, and it will also retain more heat and transmit sound. For this and other reasons it is advisable to insulate against heat and sound transference, particularly if the vessel has accommodation areas.

It is essential that insulations in the engine room and any other machinery spaces be particularly fireproof and completely incombustible. The purpose for which the vessel is designed will, to some extent, dictate the degree to which the insulation needs to be fireproof. Obviously in passenger vessels built to classification, very stringent fire precautions are laid down.

There are many materials available that will provide both acoustic and thermal insulation. These can be divided into two main types: rigid or semi-rigid panels, and spraying in situ.

Rigid or semi-rigid panels

The rigid panels are supplied as 'navy board', asbestos, polyurethane, rock wool, Dampa, Limpet boards etc. Some of them are intended for use as free standing bulkheads, linings and ceilings, and have decorative finishings bonded to the exterior. Semi-rigid panels can be obtained as rock wool, glass wool, mineral wool etc, with the different types offering varying insulating properties. They can also be obtained in thicknesses from 2.5 cm (1 in) to 10 cm (4 in), depending on the degree of insulation. They must be supported, often being fitted between structural members, and faced with a rigid lining. A typical engine room arrangement is shown in Fig 82.

FIG 82 *Fitting of insulation panels in a larger engine room.*

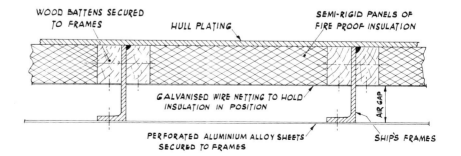

Spraying in situ

Spray insulation is marketed under several trade names. The more usual types have as their base either asbestos or polyurethane. Specialist firms with their own pump and spray units visit the vessel and, using their own specialist labour, will spray any thickness required directly on to the interior. It is advisable to etch prime (see Chapter 13) the affected area prior to spraying. This provides a key for better adhesion, and reduces the possibility of interaction with the aluminium as a result of contaminants in the spraying material. The polyurethane-type material is a two-component admix which, when mixed, produces a foaming reaction when sprayed. A good deal of overspraying takes place, so it is advisable to mask areas not to be sprayed. It is very light in weight, but care must be taken that the material is fireproof and will not give off noxious fumes when subjected to flame.

Asbestos is proof against fire, but is considerably heavier, does not have the same soundproofing qualities, and can be a health hazard if the necessary precautions are not taken to protect against disintegration and contamination.

All vessels – large and small, sail and power – should be protected against a fire hazard. The degree of protection will to a large extent depend upon the degree of risk. The high-risk areas demand the greatest protection. Wherever highly combustible fuels are used, there is a need for protection.

There are various types of extinguishant, and many are produced to deal with specific types of fire: Class A (carbonaceous material); Class B (flammable liquids); and Class C (electrical equipment). When used, they discharge a powder, gas, liquid or foam.

On smaller vessels, a few hand extinguishers located at strategic points is normally adequate. On larger vessels, a more sophisticated system should be considered.

In the high-risk areas such as the engine room, etc, a ring main consisting of stainless steel piping strategically positioned above and below the flooring, with holes drilled at intervals directed at high-risk points, is connected to the extinguishant container. The container can be discharged by mechanical/ manual operation remotely, or by automatic electrical means.

It is usual when the vessel is manned to switch the discharge to manual opera-

FIG 83 *Battery installation.*

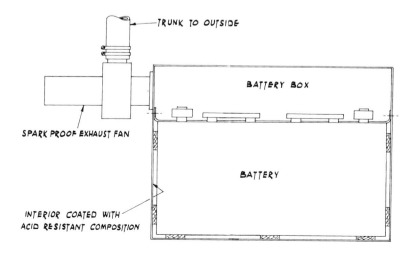

TRUNK TO OUTSIDE

BATTERY BOX

SPARK PROOF EXHAUST FAN

BATTERY

INTERIOR COATED WITH
ACID RESISTANT COMPOSITION

tion, as this reduces the risk of accidental discharge. When the vessel is unmanned it is switched to automatic.

Fire sensors are positioned strategically and connected electrically to a warning alarm and automatic control. The extinguishant used in these systems is usually an all-purpose type, either CO_2 or bromochlorodifluoromethane (BCF).

Another hazard that is often overlooked is the explosive gas given off from batteries that are being charged. In the majority of larger vessels, several banks of batteries providing light and power are being continually charged when the main or auxiliary engines are operating. This can result in an accumulation of gases that need discharging into the outside atmosphere. Where forced ventilation is used, and this is very desirable, special spark-proof gas extraction fans should be incorporated in the trunking. A typical installation is illustrated in Fig 83.

17 ◆ LAUNCHING

When the vessel is nearly complete, it has to be transferred to the water. This can be done in one of six different ways: dry dock; sideways launching; slippery ways; cradle; slings around the boat; and gunwale plates and slings.

Dry dock

If the vessel is built in a dry dock, all that is needed is to flood the dock. Normally only very large vessels are launched in this way and it is most unlikely that the type of vessel we've been considering would use this method.

Sideways launching

The vessel is placed on a framework sideways on, and close to the quay from which it is to be launched. The side of the framework farthest from the water is lifted by jacks or other means. The vessel will then slide into the water, and any inertia can be overcome by the use of force on the side by further jacks. This method is normally only used when launching into a narrow river, or where there is no slipway or lifting gear.

Slippery ways

This means that launching ways are set up, either on a slipway or on an inclined plane, consisting of a fixed portion on the ground, and a sliding portion is attached to the vessel. Between the two portions is a layer of thick grease. Initially, the sliding portion is held in position by 'dogs' which, upon being released, allow the vessel to slide into the water (see Fig 84).

Cradle

This consists of a well-braced steel framework, in one or more sections, usually set on wheels. A slipway that leads into the water is necessary. Metal rails are usually set into the slipway to receive the wheels on the cradle. These wheels may be fixed (non-swivelling) where the cradle is used only on the slipway or in a straight line, or castored (swivelling) when the cradle is used to transport the vessel around the yard. If the cradle is in one section only, it should be at least one-third the length of the vessel, and preferably longer, with poppets that sup-

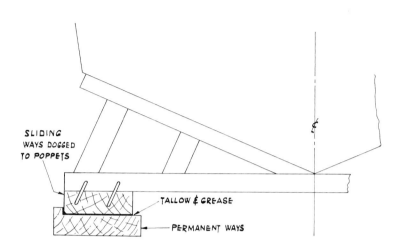

SLIDING
WAYS DOGGED
TO POPPETS

TALLOW & GREASE

PERMANENT WAYS

FIG 84 *Slippery ways.*

port the vessel placed at strategic points – ie in way of strength members such as bulkheads or deep frames (see Fig 85).

When launching into tidal waters, the cradle could be placed on the lower section of the slipway at low water, and when the tide rises the boat will float off. Discretion should be used with larger vessels because of the extra stress imposed in way of the forward poppet when the stern starts to lift. In vessels with a strong girder-like structure such as engine beds extending fore and aft and numerous stringers and reasonably calm weather conditions, no problems should be encountered. If there is any doubt, a naval architect should be consulted. A few simple calculations will indicate the degree of risk involved.

Slings

Depending on the weight of the vessel, the slings will be made either of fibre rope or flexible steel wire rope. Two slings are required, sufficiently long to go completely round the vessel, with enough extra length to reach a crane hook without too great an included angle between the forward and aft sling. Spreaders should be arranged just above the sheer between the sling legs to prevent the slings from exerting a crushing load on the hull (see Fig 86).

The crane hook will self-centre itself over the centre of gravity of the lifted weight. To ensure a level lift, the slings, if of equal length, should be positioned at equal distance forward and aft of the centre of gravity. Padding should be wrapped around the slings at points of contact with the hull to prevent damage and marking. Preventers should be secured to each sling leg around the end of the vessel, at about gunwale height, to prevent the sling from slipping inwards and so giving an unequal lift. Length of sling will also be dependent, of course, on possible maximum height of the crane hook.

Gunwale lifting plates

If the vessel needs to be lifted in and out of the water frequently, the safest and most efficient method is to fit gunwale lifting plates. These normally consist of

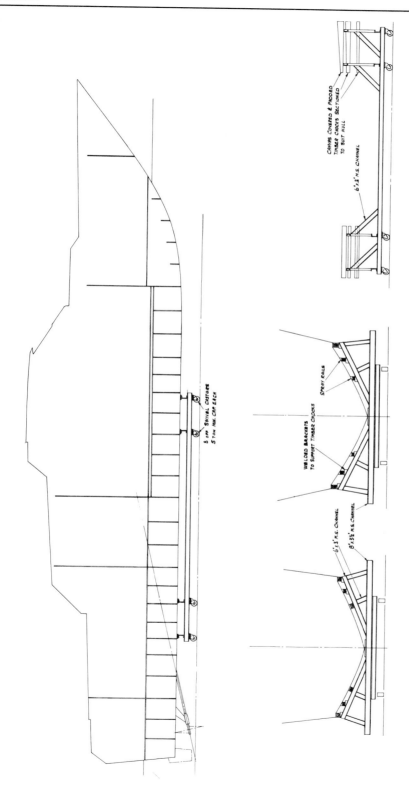

FIG 85 *Launching trolley for a 22 m (75 ft) boat.*

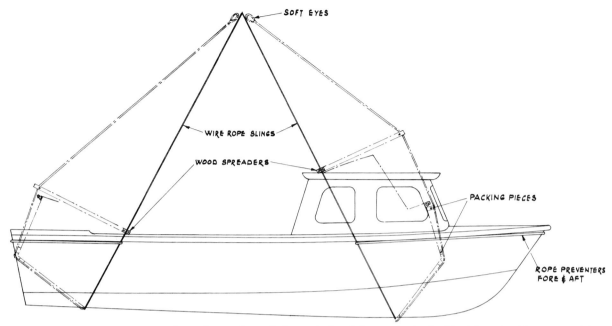

FIG 86 *Around boat slings with spreaders.*

FIG 87 *Gunwale slings.*

two- or three-legged steel plates bolted through the hull, either inside or outside, with the top of the plate extending just above the gunwale, to which the sling is attached by shackles. If possible, the plates should be positioned in way of bulkheads. If this is not possible, extra internal stiffening may be necessary to spread the stress imposed by lifting in order to avoid a stress concentration in a weak area. It is possible, of course, by having slings of unequal length, to adjust for the crane hook to come above the boat's centre of gravity and still maintain a level lift. To avoid unnecessary stress on the hull, spreaders between each sling should always be fitted for both types of slinging (see Fig 87).

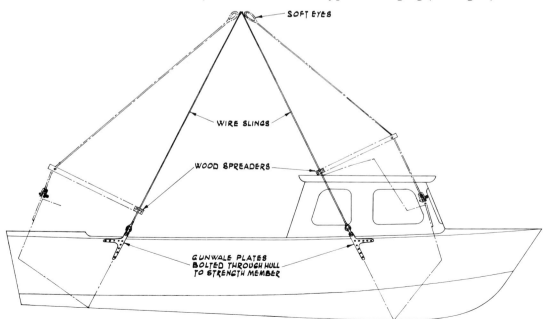

18 ◆ HULL REPAIRS

Marine-type aluminium alloys have a high degree of ductility – that is, they will deform or stretch by as much as 8–15 per cent before they rupture. Because of this, the majority of hull repairs call for the dressing of dents rather than the repair of cracks or tears.

Small indentations can be faired by the judicious use of a rubber- or hide-headed mallet, with a wooden dolly held on the opposite side. The dent should be hammered around its periphery at first, then, working in a circular direction, moved towards the centre, where the deformation is greatest.

Care must be taken not to overwork the area, as the material will work harden to the extent that it will eventually crack. When the amount of deformation is too great to respond to the above treatment, it may help to heat the area with a soft flame played around the area. The combination of heating and hammering, provided neither are used to excess, will often have the desired effect.

FIG 88 *Aluminium-hulled rigid inflatable RI22, as supplied to oil platforms in the North Sea* (Photo: David Still Ltd).

Marine-type alloys are little affected by gentle local heat, but (unlike steel) do not change colour when heated. This makes it harder to control the heat if you're not sure of the temperature of the affected zone. To give an indication of this, it is advisable to use temperature indicating crayons of about 204°C (400°F) and 260°C (500°F). Circles close to the centre of the deformation should be marked with the 260°C (500°F) crayon and rings outside this central zone should be marked with the 204°C (400°F) crayon. Heat should be applied until the crayon marks start to melt, then remove the heat and commence hammering. Further heating and hammering should be kept to a minimum.

When the fairing has been completed, the area should be cooled with a light douche of water. Where a very fair hull is required, as for instance on the bottom of racing hulls, slight depressions can be faired by the application of an epoxy resin such as Araldite. The metal must be degreased, abraded with emery cloth, and then degreased again. Mixing and application should be to the manufacturer's instructions.

Several thin coats should be applied in preference to a few thick coats. Curing can be accelerated by heating; when fully cured, the surface sets rock hard and can be sanded to a very fine smooth finish.

Where the metal has actually torn, leaving a jagged edge, the metal should be dressed back as far as possible to the original shape. The area of the tear should be cut out, including a generous margin all round, to ensure that any surface cracks that could propagate are removed, and a patch should be welded in position. When any doubt exists about the integrity of the metal local to the repair, an interior doubler can be welded in position to cover the doubtful area (Fig 89). When the damaged plate is too thin for welding, or the welding facility is not available, the patch can be riveted in position (Fig 90). For all underwater

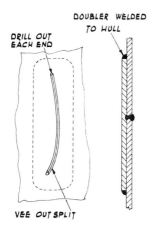

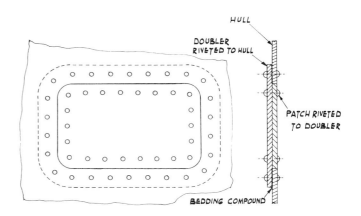

FIG 89 Left: *Interior doubler welded to hull over split.*

FIG 90 Right: *Patch riveted when welding facility is not available.*

riveting, solid rivets or the sealed type should be used, and all mating surfaces and rivet shanks should be coated with a suitable elastomer sealant. Where a very heavy blow has been sustained covering a large area, it is not often that an actual split in the metal will occur as a result of overstretching. Because of the extreme ductility there is more likely to be an excessive stretching of the metal. This tends to inhibit its return to the original shape, there being more area than originally. Where the damaged plate is not replaced, it may be necessary to saw a slot in the centre of the dent. This provides room for metal displacement during the fairing process. The width of the slot will vary with the amount of stretching that has occurred.

One advantage with an aluminium hull is that, where a permanent set has occurred, the aluminium work hardens because of the distortion and its strength increases. Further loading up to the amount that caused the original deformation will not result in further distortion because the metal is not weakened by the effect of stretching.

If the interior structure has suffered excessive damage, this should be replaced rather than repaired. It is more difficult to 'lose' metal in extrusions than plate and, being usually a harder material, it will tend to resist re-forming.

19 ◆ UNIT CONSTRUCTION

In the context of the scope of this book, unit construction means the construction of parts of a boat separately, say up to about five parts, to make it easier for a small yard to take on the production of a boat that under normal construction methods they would be unable to undertake – or at least find very difficult. For

FIG 91 Above left: (a) *Assembly of the keel, set on a keel jig, of a 35 m (114 ft) motor yacht. Note the flat strip on the interior stiffeners to accommodate the plug welds on final assembly plating.* Above right: (b) *The whole of the forepart is made up as a separate unit. Spaces must be provided during the plating to enable the welder to tack weld the frames in position.* Below left: (c) *The forward sections, having been separately made up, are assembled on the midship section.* Below right: (d) *The base of the aft section is lifted into position; bulkheads and frames will follow prior to final plating.*

larger yards where this stricture does not apply, they may even find it more cost effective to adopt this form of construction.

In the normal way, vessels up to about 25 m (82 ft) are constructed from scratch as a whole unit. They are built up gradually, with the labour force increasing as the job progresses so that more people are employed over the period of construction. With unit construction, the total labour force can be employed from the start, thus making for a more concentrated effort that will reduce the overall building time. The available floor space is also used more effectively, and in cutting down the size of each unit piece there is probably less time spent climbing about on staging. A little more time may need to be spent on jig building, but this is nothing compared with the benefits.

The photographs in this chapter illustrate a 35 m (114 ft) twin screw motor yacht being constructed by this method. Fig 91(a) shows the keel being plated up. As can be seen, one side is space welded to the stiffeners and the closing side would be plug welded, ie slots cut in the plate in way of the stiffeners and inside edges of the plate welded to the stiffeners. A very careful watch must be kept on the straightness of the keel during construction and any deviation corrected before continuing. Part of the bottom, up to the lower deck, will usually be constructed upside down, the keel assembled, and the bottom plating fitted. In Fig 91(b) the stem and forepeak has been framed and is being plated. Fig 91(c) shows assembly of the forepart and the top sides are being added. In Fig 91(d) the afterpart has been lifted into position, and the bulkheads are being assembled. Once the hull has been totally assembled, the vessel will be in a position to be launched for towing away to the fitting out yard.

20 ◆ DESIGNING STRUCTURES IN ALUMINIUM ALLOYS

by Tony Marchant

Aluminium alloys are a popular choice for the construction of all types of marine vessels and structures, mainly because of their excellent corrosion resistance, together with low weight and ease of joining by welding. There is a wide choice of plate thicknesses made from the non-heat-treatable alloys, and many extruded sections are made from heat-treatable alloys. Furthermore, the material is easily worked and, as no expensive tooling is needed (in contrast to that required by fibre reinforced polymers), vessels manufactured in single units are cost competitive.

The physical and mechanical properties of the more commonly used alloys for marine vessels and structures are shown in Table 1.

Non-heat-treatable alloys containing magnesium are the 5000 series and they are available in sheet, plate and shate form. Some simply shaped extrusions are also available in these alloys. The strength of the alloy increases by work hardening, but the strength reverts back to that of the annealed property when welded.

Heat-treatable alloys, containing magnesium and silicon, are the 6000 series and they are available in extruded sections as well as sheet and plate. The 700 series, containing added copper, provide the highest strength alloy, but they are not suitable for welding and they have a lower corrosion resistance than the 6000 series.

There is therefore a wide selection of alloys available, but the more commonly available materials are 5083 and 6082 in various degrees of cold working and heat treatment.

To put aluminium alloy into perspective with other materials, Table 2 compares its principal mechanical properties with those of other materials commonly used for constructing marine vessels.

It is interesting to compare the specific strength and stiffness values – ie the tensile strength and modulus divided by the density of the material. It can be seen that aluminium alloy compares with steel for stiffness, but is superior with respect to specific tensile strength. This indicates that any well-designed structure in aluminium alloy will be lighter than a steel structure. It also compares well with glass-reinforced polyester, being particularly superior in stiffness. The more expensive high-performance carbon-reinforced epoxy cannot, however, be matched by any steel or alloy.

Design philosophy

The importance of a good and thorough design philosophy cannot be overemphasised. All structures need to be carefully designed to ensure compliance with operating parameters, to reduce weight to a minimum, and to keep building

TABLE 1 *Typical physical and mechanical properties of commercially available alloys taken from* The Properties of Aluminium and its Alloys, *Aluminium Federation.*

Material designation and temper	Density g/cm^3	Coefficient of linear expansion (10^{-6}/°C) (20–100°C)	0.2% proof stress MPa	Tensile strength MPa	Shear strength MPa	Fatigue strength MPa (50×10^6Hz)	Modulus of elasticity GPa	Hardness		
								Brinell	Vickers	Rockwell B
5083 0	2.67	24.5	140	312	155	124	69	72	76	–
5083 H22	2.67	24.5	250	337	–	–	69	95	100	52.8
5083 H24	2.67	24.5	285	375	–	–	69	110	116	63.6
5251 0	2.69	24.0	87	180	125	92	70	45	47	–
5251 H22	2.69	24.0	150	220	–	124	70	62	65	–
5251 H24	2.69	24.0	190	250	139	–	70	70	74	–
5454 0	2.69	24.0	100	250	159	–	70	62	65	–
5454 H22	2.69	24.0	200	277	165	–	70	73	77	–
5454 H24	2.69	24.0	225	297	179	–	70	81	85	–
6061 T4	2.70	24.0	125	215	165	95	69	60–70	64–74	–
6061 T6	2.70	24.0	265	305	205	95	69	90–100	95–105	48–56.6
6063 T4	2.70	24.0	90	155	131	79	69	48	50	–
6063 T6	2.70	23.5	180	210	155	85	69	75	79	–
6082 T4	2.70	23.0	130	225	178	106	69	60–70	64–74	–
6082 T6	2.70	23.0	270	310	218	124	69	90–100	95–105	48–56.5
7075 T6	2.80	23.5	495	565	330	–	72	150	–	–

costs as low as possible. None of this can be achieved by guessing sizes and quantities of materials. It is therefore necessary to do calculations to establish the scantlings for the structure.

There are two approaches that can be used to obtain scantlings. The first is to use the empirical data laid down by the classification societies, such as Lloyd's Register of Shipping,[1] Det Norske Veritas, American Bureau of Shipping, and Bureau Veritas. The so called rules of these classification societies provide the primary scantlings of aluminium alloy vessels based on many years of experience. However, it must be remembered that these rules are based on empirical data, so if optimum weight is sought then a 'first principle' calculation approach must be used. All the classification societies will accept such an approach by the submission of calculations and relevant drawings.

The advantage of a first principle approach is that all areas of detail can be covered, an important factor because generally it is the detail area of the structure that can cause problems. Where a particular type of vessel is not covered by classification, or indeed classification approval is not required, then a first principle approach is the preferred route.

TABLE 2 *Comparative properties of aluminium alloys with steels and FRP*

Property	Steel		FRP		Al. Aloy	
	Mild steel	High yield steel	E glass (WR) reinforced polyester	Carbon (WR) reinforced epoxy	5083	
					welded	unwelded
Tensile strength (MPa)	430–540	620	228	550	312	375
Yield strength (MPa)	255	550	–	–	140	285
Compression strength (MPa)	–	–	186	360	–	–
Tensile modulus of elasticity (GPa)	207	207	13.8	55	69	69
Density (g/cm³)	7.8	7.8	1.63	1.47	2.67	2.67
Specific tensile strength (MPa/g/cm³)	62	79.5	140	374	117	140
Specific tensile modulus of elasticity (GPa/g/cm³)	26.5	26.5	8.5	37	26	26
Fibre weight fraction (%)	–	–	50	59	–	–

FIG 92 *A 41 m (134 ft) monohull fast passenger vessel in operation in Italian waters. Specially designed for coastal and inshore routes with low-wash characteristics* (Photo: FBM Marine Ltd).

Design loads and factors of safety

The type of boat or vessel being considered will determine the principal loads subjected to the structure. Sailing yachts are generally concerned with local and overall stiffness, together with the loading from the rigging. Power craft operating over 25 knots will be dominated by the wave-slamming forces. Larger vessels (eg fast ferries) will be designed for slamming forces, hydrostatic pressures and overall (global) loads due to bending and torsion.

The derivation of these loads can be obtained from some of the classification rules;[1] these give wave-slamming pressures, together with recommendations for deck loadings, green sea pressures and stiffness criteria. A useful approach for obtaining wave-slamming pressures can be gleaned from the published data of Savitsky and Ward Brown,[2] used in conjunction with the work of Allen and Jones.[3]

Factors of safety are chosen against a number of parameters, including the nature of the load (short or long term), the confidence in the loading data, the expected quality of manufacture, and the extent of the calculations. The classification societies select factors of safety for various areas of structure and different loading criteria. Where classification does not govern the design, the designer is free to select the factors of safety. Generally speaking, commercial craft are designed using a factor of 1.5 on slamming pressures and 3 to 4 for deck loads and hydrostatic pressures.

Where weight is to be reduced to an absolute minimum, for instance in performance sailing yachts and racing powercraft, then the factor of safety could be as low as 1.0 on yield where there is a high degree of confidence in the loading data.

Structural configuration

The purpose of any vessel structure is to define the hydrodynamic and aerodynamic profile, to provide the supporting surfaces for the payload and, of course, provide a watertight envelope. The generated external surface area will form a major percentage of the overall weight and therefore it is desirable to keep the 'shell' plating thickness down to a practical minimum – ie one which, for the hull, will not fracture on impact with floating debris or be insufficiently robust in the superstructure to have an adequate lifespan. Classification rules are a useful guide to the practical minimum plating thicknesses, basing the value on the materials' strength, the vessel size and the various locations throughout the structure.

The plating, then, needs support, first by local stiffeners running on to frames, which can be either longitudinal or transverse, with the type and size of the vessel generally dictating the framing direction. The importance of adequate load paths must be carefully addressed, for all loads must have somewhere to go into the structure. Welding is the most commonly used method of joining as it is less expensive than riveting. However, the welded area will be reduced in strength and care is needed in designing welded structures to avoid unnecessary stress concentrations.

A typical stiffener plate using welded angle bars is shown in Fig 93. The pitch and size of the stiffeners is determined by calculation for the pressure on the plating. The design must allow for the reduced material strength in the welded zone, which in this case is at the plating to stiffener interface. The weld there-

FIG 93 *A typical stiffened plate configuration.*

fore reduces the overall performance of the structure. To overcome this, an extruded shape can be used, as shown in Fig 94.

FIG 94 *An extruded section used for plating.*

The size of any extrusion is governed by the capacity of the extruder. Typically, the sections used for plating would be extruded up to between 50–60 cm (approx 19–23 in) in width, but much will depend on the selected shape.

The weld is now away from the stiffener and therefore the parent material strength can be used as opposed to the welded strength. Further 'tricks' can be played with the weld to reduce the effect on the structure. For instance, if the weld is moved away from the centre of the shell plating panel where high bending stresses will develop, towards the point of contraflexure (zero bending moment), then the panel will be more efficient (see Fig 95).

FIG 95 *A weld placed at the point of zero bending moment.*

A further advantage of the purpose-designed extrusions is that they can be welded using automatic welding equipment, giving a higher quality of weld than that achieved by hand welding. The joined extrusions are then presented to the vessel framing for assembly. However, double curvature is difficult to achieve by this method and a compromise in geometry may have to be obtained to achieve an acceptable cost performance from the structure.

Extruded shapes can be further optimised by using closed sections. Fig 96 shows a purpose-designed section for a fast-ferry structure, which has been optimised for the bending and shear stresses induced by slamming pressures. Note that the weld is placed away from the centre of the plate. The various thicknesses of the extrusions can be carefully controlled, together with the overall geometry.

By moving from the all-welded structure shown in Fig 93 to that shown in Fig 96, between 10 and 15 per cent of weight can be saved. This therefore highlights the design philosophy of first principle calculation.

Of course elimination of the weld itself provides a benefit, and this can be done by using mechanical fasteners such as rivets. It can also be achieved by the use of suitable adhesives and this is an area that is receiving a great deal of attention.

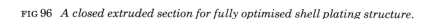

FIG 96   *A closed extruded section for fully optimised shell plating structure.*

The analysis of the shell plating itself needs to recognise the flexibility of the plating, which is likely to be relatively thin compared to the span. Plates that have a deflection of more than half their thickness become affected by the membrane stresses developed, and therefore normal bending theory no longer applies. Isotropic non-linear plates, such as aluminium alloy, can be designed using the charts of the Engineering Sciences Data Unit (ESDU).[4] Plates in bending, together with many other useful formulae, can be found in ROARK, *Formulas for Stress and Strain.*[5]

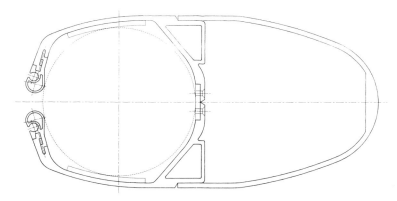

FIG 97   *A purpose designed yacht mast* (Sparcraft Europe Ltd).

A particularly good example of using extrusions for optimum geometric and structural performance is the modern yacht mast. Fig 97 illustrates the benefits that can be obtained by incorporating into the section the cavity for the roller furling mainsail and the aft luff slot. The various extrusions are bonded and screwed together; this provides the overall bending and torsional stiffness required, while maintaining adequate margins of strength.

FIG 98 *Typical sandwich structures incorporating aluminium alloy facing skins.*

Sandwich structures utilise bonding agents to fix the facing skins to the selected core material and the resulting structures provide another useful way of weight saving. Fig 98 illustrates the typical materials used.

Aluminium alloy skins bonded to aluminium honeycomb of various cell sizes and thicknesses.

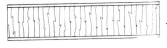

Aluminium alloy skins bonded to end balsa wood.

Aluminium alloy skins bonded to PVC foams of varying densities.

In summary, designing in aluminium alloy must be an integrated function with production instigated at the very start of a project. Retrospective design leads to unacceptable compromises and increased costs.

Aluminium alloy offers the designer the ability to tailor the sections for structures of optimum weight and cost. Limited tooling only is needed to build a vessel that puts aluminium alloy in a class of its own when it comes to lightweight cost-effective marine structures.

References

1 *Provisional Rules for the Classification of High Speed Catamarans*, Lloyd's Register of Shipping, 1991; *Tentative Rules for the Classification of High Speed and Light Craft*, Det Norske Veritas Classification A/S, 1991.

2 'Procedures for hydrodynamic evaluation of planing hulls in smooth and rough water', D Savitsky and P Ward Brown, *Marine Technology*, Vol 13, No 4, Oct 1976, pp. 381–400.

3 *A Simplified Method of Determining Structural Design – Limit Pressures on High Performance Marine Vehicles*, R G Allen and R R Jones, AIAA/SNAME Advanced Marine Vehicles Conference, 1978.

4 *Elastic Direct Stresses and Deflections for Flat Rectangular Plates under Uniformly Distributed Pressure*, Engineering Sciences Data Unit, Item 7013.

5 *Formulas for Stress and Strain*, ROARK, McGraw-Hill.

21 ◆ Racing powerboats

by John Walker

Of all the world's major boatbuilding markets currently favouring aluminium –
eg custom yachts, commercial and work boats, racing sail boats and racing
powerboats – it is the last category that has seen alloys engineered to their greatest advantage. If we look at the way the sport of offshore powerboat racing has
developed, then it is easy to see why this is so.

When leisure boating emerged from the shadows of the Second World War,
naval architects and boatbuilders worked initially in wood and later in the newly
emerging glass reinforced plastic. While builders in northern Europe polarised
towards well found but modestly performing cruisers, their opposite numbers in
Italy and North America were servicing home markets that had traditionally

FIG 99 *Gas-turbine-engined race boat travelling at about 80 mph.*

demanded more open and faster craft. That quest, which continues to this day, took three primary and important courses: evolving hull design and structure, enhanced mechanical performance, and building materials.

If nothing else, the war wonderfully concentrated the minds of designers and builders on the subject of improving the performance of powered craft – not just in speed, but in their ability to maintain higher speeds in open seaways. By the mid-1950s designers such as Ray Hunt were pursuing alternative underwater shapes, and the first major breakthrough came with his development of a full planing hull.

Gone was the vertical entry, flatter aft sections and round bilges of earlier displacement craft. In their place, Hunt developed a raked stem running aft from deep- to medium-vee sections, hard chines and a vertical transom; it was not long before a succession of boatbuilders took up his new designs, with an increasing number of them producing vessels made of GRP.

Gaining market advantage by competitive success was in no way a new concept so the advent of modern offshore racing in 1958 proved to be an attractive proposition for the likes of cruiser builders Bertram, Chris Craft, Donzi and Formula. The development of GRP allowed builders to offer race proving as part of the sales package.

FIG 100 *The 9.7 m (32 ft) all-welded Maritime hull was built in Florida to a Wynne Walters design for the season of 1965. Fitted with war surplus gas turbines and later petrol engines,* Thunderbird *became the first aluminium hull to win an offshore powerboat race* (Photo: EyeSea Library).

By the early 1960s GRP monohulls, powered largely by American 8 V petrol motors, were dominating offshore racing in the United States and Europe, and developments of Hunt's deep-vee concept were being built in both Italy and Britain. However, there was already a move to investigate alloy as a viable material alongside wood and plastic for fast-boat construction.

In 1963 Hampshire builder A E Freezer commissioned and fabricated a 7 m

(23 ft) design from the board of Dennis Palmer. Two years later, an American, Merrick Lewis, built the 9.7 m (32 ft) *Maritime* to a design of Jim Wynne and Walt Walters – in this instance, an all-welded deep-vee construction. The boat, with its unique gas turbine power, made history in the United States by not just starting the tough Miami–Nassau marathon race, but actually *winning* it.

Lewis set the fashion trend for spectacular machine-turned decks and topsides, but more importantly the alloy boat held together when driven very hard in rough conditions and became the first aluminium hull to find competitive success anywhere in the world in the modern sport.

For the 1966 Cowes–Torquay race Peter Du Cane designed a 11.5 m (38 ft) monohull to carry two 650 hp Daytona petrol inboards, and had utilised all the inherent weight-saving potential of aluminium to produce a spectacularly light craft. Of an all-welded construction, the builders Vosper overcame the flexibility of lightweight, thinner gauge topside and deck plating by swaging their forward sections into regular longitudinal corrugations to aft of the midships station. While this corrugation technique stiffened up the plates, there was pre-season concern over the potential working of riveted plates and fatigue cracking in the after sections of the hull.

FIG 101 *Designer Don Shead opted for swaged and riveted topsides and deck plating on the 9.9 m (32 ft 6 in)* Miss Enfield 2, *the Mercruiser-powered monohull that carried Sopwith, Shead and de Selincourt into the runner-up spot in the 1970 World Championship and broke the grip of the United States and GRP on Class I hulls* (Photo: EyeSea Library).

Whether from this or other damage, the highly competitive *Flying Fish* opened up and foundered in the heavy seas of Lyme Bay; this encouraged designers to take a longer look at aluminium and how best to employ it. While structural failures were not unique to the comparatively rare alloy boats, that rarity ensured that they were more closely scrutinised and reported.

Designers were polarised in their thinking about aluminium, with some believing that it was only good for giving additional strength to more conventional materials, and others convinced that if aluminium suppliers could develop plate, bar and section to withstand the chemical reaction with sea and air, structure could be devised to maximise its weight-saving potential.

While aluminium continued to be favoured by a few American race boatbuilders, the year 1969 turned out to be a watershed in the wider acceptability and development of the material, for it marked an awakening interest by emergent designer Don Shead.

Driven by Tommy Sopwith, a 7.6 m (25 ft) wooden built Shead design had won the rough water Cowes race of 1968 watched by Greek shipping heir John Goulandris. Already the owner of a shipyard on the Isle of Wight and committed to aluminium as a building material, he contacted the winning team and offered them his help in developing an aluminium race boat to compete at international level.

FIG 102 *Don Shead's early work with Enfield Marine led to a succession of world-beating monohulls from the Italian yard of Cantieri Uniti Viareggio. Initially of 11.2 m (37 ft), the same basic design was ultimately stretched to 12.4 m (41 ft), and diesel-powered examples such as* Follett *were still winning championships as recently as 1989* (Photo: EyeSea Library/Walker).

While Sopwith's win in this most prestigious race was in a Class II boat, Goulandris had bigger plans for the Class I World Championship circuit and commissioned Shead to produce a design to exploit the advantages of alloy with that in mind. In retrospect, Shead's work in 1969 and 1970 was seminal in the development of aluminium in fast powerboats, and his rapid grasp of its engineering properties and their application was to dominate offshore racing for the next decade.

His first design for Goulandris' Enfield Marine was the 10 m (33 ft) monohull, *Miss Enfield.* Shead had raced alongside both American- and British-built aluminium boats in the mid 1960s and had observed their advantages and problems at first hand. Initially, he rejected swaging and riveting, opting instead for an all-welded construction that was less elegant than functional. At first glance, the new aluminium craft was similar in thinking to conventional light wooden boats, but there were a number of differences.

Most obvious was Shead's motor installation, for the first time designed around the highly successful Mercruiser inboard/outdrive configuration. The second difference was that while Shead perfectly understood the limit of marine plywood, having worked with it since he entered racing, and while the properties of aluminium were well enough documented, their application was an unknown quantity. Plate gauges, extruded channel sections, the number and positioning of frames and indeed welding techniques, were all experimental.

As an engineer, however, he understood the benefits of simple solutions and synergic materials, so although *Miss Enfield* looked arguably a little agricultural with her slabby topsides and flat deck, her underwater shape was well proven. Shead also designed items such as the fuel catch tank and water ballast tank in alloy; but one exception was his choice of butyl rubber for the fuel tanks themselves, thus mirroring racing car practice.

FIG 103 Blitz *after crashing into the rocks at a reputed 70 mph.*

Enfield's second boat, *Miss Enfield 2*, retained the fully welded construction of its underwater sections below the chine, but opted for the potentially lighter swaged and riveted topsides and deck. This produced a much stiffer design and, in so doing, effectively shaped aluminium race boat construction techniques for twenty years. Coincidentally, it also moved British builders of race boats into a position of pre-eminence in the sport.

A succession of projects followed from Enfield and Shead. All employed the proven format of welding below the chines and riveting swaged plates above, notably the experimental 10.3 m (34 ft) catamaran *Ali-Cat*, the 11.2 m (37 ft) *Enfield Avenger* and, before the yard turned its attention exclusively to building larger commercial craft, a sister boat for Italian water jet manufacturers, Castoldi.

Possibly as a result of this introduction, but more probably through Shead's own successful racing exploits, a number of Italian drivers began to express interest in aluminium as an alternative to the ranks of GRP boats coming out of Florida. That interest resulted in contracts to build a range of 11.2–12.4 m (37–41 ft) monohulls in the Mediterranean port of Viareggio.

The well-established Picchiotti shipyard undertook the first of these, but because of pressure of work they promptly subcontracted the building to a smaller yard, Cantieri Uniti Viareggio. That boat and subsequent follow-on orders positioned CUV as Europe's premier builder of aluminium monohulls.

By the late 1970s, at about the same time that the American stranglehold on offshore racing was being broken by CUV in Italy, it was under increasing pressure from another direction too. The traditional monohull was being consistently outperformed by a newer breed of offshore catamarans.

FIG 104 *Modern state-of-the art catamarans are mostly jigged and fabricated upside down.* (Photo: EyeSea Library/Cougar).

In themselves, catamaran designs were not new, and indeed catamarans had been used experimentally in offshore racing for many years. But the leading edge technology came from British builders Cougar, whose multihull designs had been successful in circuit racing and had begun to make their presence felt in the smaller offshore classes. Their background experience and a perceived need to be able to vary underwater geometry had persuaded them to persevere with wood.

In 1977 evolution in structure, size and hydrodynamics came together in their first Class I catamaran and its potential made it impossible to ignore, particularly in the United States. In the face of an offshore catamaran that would regularly top the magic 100 mph barrier, there were few remaining competitive drivers happy to plod around at 90 mph – the theoretical limit of stability and safety for equivalent-sized monohulls.

Cougar's move into aluminium was quick and effective. In 1978 a 9.7 m (32 ft) catamaran design was built under subcontract, and within two years they had both catamarans and monohulls under construction in alloy in Europe and the

FIG 105 *Cougar's first aluminium catamaran was subcontracted and built by Sims Aluminium Ltd to their lines. As an experiment, the 9.7 m (32 ft) Romans Sabre was remarkably successful but lacked lift – regularly popping frames and welds in the forward sections of the flat running hulls* (Photo: EyeSea Library/Cougar).

United States to supply an expanding market in Class I and the bigger US Superboat class.

Early fears for the seakeeping capability of catamarans in rough water, and worries about structures surviving the high speed and often uneven shock loadings inevitable when running hard, were eventually overcome. And, despite the fact that wooden catamarans were still demonstrably lighter and therefore faster, one of the major selling points for aluminium boats was their ability to survive

TABLE 3 *Comparative weights of race boats in aluminium, GRP and FRP indicate dramatic improvements over twenty years of structural and fabrication development*

Boatbuilder	Hull type	Build year	Building material	Overall length in m (ft)	Weight in kg (lb)	Type of building
Cigarette	Mono	1969	GRP	10.9 (36)	2903 (6400)	Moulded
Enfield Marine	Mono	1970	ALU	9.9 (32½)	2495 (5500)	Swage/rivet
Cougar Marine	Mono	1984	ALU	14 (46)	2268 (5000)	Swage/rivet
Cougar Marine	Mono	1985	GRP	10 (33)	1769 (3900)	Moulded
Cougar Marine	Mono	1986	GRP	14 (46)	2585 (5700)	Moulded
CUV	Mono	1988	ALU	12.4 (41)	3220 (7100)	Swage/rivet
Cougar Marine	Mono	1991	FRP	14 (46)	2155 (4750)	Moulded
Enfield Marine	Cat	1970	ALU	10.3 (34)	3436 (7575)	Swage/rivet
Cougar Marine	Cat	1990	ALU	11.5 (38)	2540 (5600)	Swage/rivet
Codecasa Due	Cat	1990	ALU	13.7 (45)	2177 (4800)	Weld/glue
Douglas Skater	Cat	1991	FRP	12.8 (42)	2268 (5000)	Moulded

Weights are approximate for hull, deck and tanks, but exclude all equipment and protect their occupants better in the event of accidents – particularly the potentially lethal high-speed trip and submarine stuff.

The success of the catamaran in offshore racing was rapid and dramatic, and within their first decade of acceptance catamarans had won the World Championship on five occasions. All of them were Cougars and all of them were aluminium but, having once been in a unique position of dominance, the British builders now found themselves in competition with at least five European yards (including CUV) and as many again in the United States. Despite the proliferation of marques and designs and, more importantly, in the face of other materials such as FRP and composites, aluminium still retains its appeal.

Having looked at the background to aluminium's place in offshore racing, we must now turn at its applied technology and use.

Initially, aluminium was investigated for its potential to save weight without devaluing structural integrity. More recently, designers have been utilising the engineering potential of alloys. Table 3 reveals just how much has been achieved in twenty years of competition.

Early all-welded aluminium construction did not exploit its weight-saving potential to its sensible limits, but it was relatively simple and easy to fabricate, and it demonstrated a saving of 10–12 per cent over conventionally moulded GRP craft. Plate welds were efficient in maintaining structural efficacy and did not require further sealing to prevent the ingress of water, which was an immediate problem for riveted constructions.

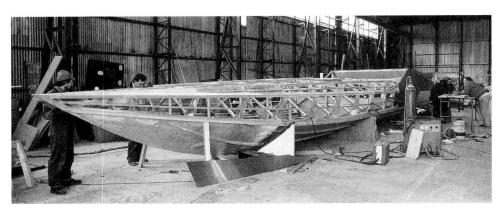

FIG 106 *When Cougar began building their own aluminium hulls it was the US1-46 monohull that became favoured by American Superboat competitors. A radical rethink of conventional structures produced the efficient vertical and diagonal compression poles with their attendant lighter weight* (Photo: EyeSea Library/Cougar).

Early swaged and riveted constructions produced weight savings in the order of 15–18 per cent over GRP mouldings, but later monohulls built using essentially the same techniques have shown a constant improvement. This is perhaps best illustrated by comparing Enfield Marine's first swaged and riveted race boat from 1970, a vessel 9.9 m (32½ ft) with a dry weight of 2495 kg (5500 lb), with Cougar Marine's ostensibly similarly constructed Superboat design of 1984, a boat of 14 m (46 ft) weighing a mere 2268 kg (5000 lb).

Early aluminium structures mirrored traditional practice in wood by employing conventionally placed frames and bulkheads. Cougar's breakthrough came with the total respecification of accepted structures that relied on compression tubes mounted vertically between keel band and deck beams, linked to similar tubes running diagonally outboard from deck beams to chines.

The reduction in structural weight, allied to the immense strength that the tubular form provided, allowed a reduction in plate gauges and frames. Further weight reduction came from chopping out extraneous metal in all areas, but particularly from frames, bulkheads and engine bearers. While losing none of its craft skills, the building of race boats had made the transition from traditional marine practice to techniques more akin to aircraft construction.

It is interesting to note that given sufficient time and manpower to develop a concept fully, well planned alloy construction in an identical design can achieve close to the saving achieved by modern FRP composites and Kevlar over conventionally moulded GRP.

Pursuing a similar tubular structure in catamarans produced predictable weight saving, but in boats that are now regularly expected to travel at speeds of over 125 mph in open seas, weight saving is not in itself the total recipe for success – although having weight in hand is unbeatable. The equation is simply that for any given available power, the lighter the boat the longer can be its overall and therefore its waterline length, and the benefit of that has never been in doubt.

Taking offshore racing's 16 litre Class I between 1970 and 1992 as the working example, maximum speeds have increased from around 75 mph to around 125 mph or 67 per cent, while boat lengths have increased from around 9.7 m (32 ft) to 13.7 m (45 ft) or 40 per cent. Clearly, engine development has been easier than hull development, which inevitably has still to work within the parameters of its seaborne environment, but the search for strength and stiffness continues.

Current practice varies between those builders who achieve stiffness by tying in the frames to longitudinals and rider bars and those who let their frames float within the overall structure. Typically, today's race boats have 2 mm ($\frac{1}{12}$ in) topsides and 1.6 mm (just over $\frac{1}{16}$ in) deck plates, but there are different technologies under consideration. The most important of these is the combination of conventional welding with modern adhesives, a practice that (although comparatively new in racing powerboats) has been present in such applications as hovercraft since the 1970s.

Typically these new designs are welded from chine to chine through the wet-deck tunnel area and have bulkheads and frames welded to all longitudinals, but adhesives are used to secure topside and upper deck plates. No builder has yet had the confidence to rely solely on adhesives, but such are the properties of modern room temperature or controlled warm cure epoxy or epoxy/acrylic glues that plate gauges and rivet numbers can be substantially reduced, giving additional weight saving. Even with modern superglues, locking skin panels with rivets is still recommended as it helps to minimise the problem of plate peeling.

Where peel is the predominant load on a joint, designing to place it under tensile stress improves its performance. Considerable advantage can be obtained by substituting the standard weld joint by bonding: notably, not having to subject the base material to very high temperatures with attendant changes in its microstructure, distortion or fatigue potential. Adhesives also fulfil the function of sealants. Glue bonding can also improve stiffness over welded or riveted joints, but weight reduction appears to have been as important in its early specification for race boats.

Table 3 shows that, comparatively, a 13.7 m (45 ft) catamaran from Codecasa

FIG 107 *Two decades of design development have carried the catamaran from circuit racing lightweight to total dominance in offshore sport. Capable of running hard in heavy weather, today's cat driver sits strapped within a canopied cockpit and must be prepared to run at speeds approaching 120 mph to be competitive* (Photo: Colin Taylor Productions).

Due, making wide use of adhesive technology, has shown a weight saving of around 17 per cent over a state of the art 11.5 m (38 ft) design from Cougar Marine, and a reduction in topside plating from 2 mm ($\frac{1}{12}$ in) to 1.2 mm (just over $\frac{1}{20}$ in) and in deck plating from 1.6 mm (just over $\frac{1}{16}$ in) to 1 mm ($\frac{1}{24}$ in). That same technology has allowed reduced frame size and spacing, while bonding and riveting all sides of the plates to both frames and longitudinals can reduce racking and distortion under twist loading. Thus a 25 per cent weight saving is a real possibility.

In practical application, working with adhesives has its problems – most notably, welding repairs in the proximity of bonded joints because the heating process can destroy the bond. The extent of such destruction is purely a function of time and temperature, but experiments would seem to indicate that 30 seconds at temperatures up to 275°C (527°F) is about the limit. However, a well-designed bonded joint will spread loads over the entire surface of the bond, and is likely to maintain its structural efficacy beyond failure of the base material that it is bonding together.

Aluminium has taken its rightful place as today's preferred building material for race boats in all classes and has advanced from all-welding through swage and rivet to weld and adhesive. But what of the future? In the face of Kevlar, carbon fibre and composites, the search for strength and lightness may lead designers toward lithium and titanium as alternatives, but highly specialised welding techniques and an increase by as much as 150 per cent in material costs alone make it seem likely that aluminium will be the material that carries the sport through its next decade.

INDEX

OTHER TITLES AVAILABLE FROM ADLARD COLES NAUTICAL

☐	Complete Amateur Boat Building 4th Edition	£17.95
☐	Boat Electrical Systems	£12.99
☐	Propeller Handbook	£17.99
☐	Boatowner's Mechanical and Electrical Manual	£30.00
☐	Metal Corrosion in Boats	£11.99
☐	Designer's Notebook 2nd Edition	£5.99
☐	Fitting Out 4th Edition	£9.99
☐	Laying Up Your Boat	£7.99
☐	101 Tips and Hints for Your Boat	£7.99

All these books are available or can be ordered from your local bookshop or can be ordered direct from the publisher. Simply tick the titles you want and fill in the form below.

Prices and availability subject to change without notice.

Adlard Coles Nautical Cash Sales, PO Box 11, Falmouth, Cornwall TR10 9EN.

Please send a cheque or postal order for the value of the book and add the following for postage and packing.

UK including BFPO: £1.00 for one book plus 50p for the second book and 30p for each additional book ordered up to a £3.00 maximum.

OVERSEAS INCLUDING EIRE: £2.00 for the first book, plus £1.00 for the second book, and 50p for each additional book ordered.

OR Please debit this amount from my Access/Visa Card (delete as appropriate).

Card number ☐☐☐☐☐☐☐☐☐☐☐☐☐☐☐☐

Amount £ ....

Expiry date ....

Signed ....

Name ....

Address ....

....

Fax no: 0326 376423